The Politician by James Shirley

A TRAGEDY. Presented at Salisbury Court by Her Majesties Servants

James Shirley was born in London in September 1596.

His education was through a collection of England's finest establishments: Merchant Taylors' School, London, St John's College, Oxford, and St Catharine's College, Cambridge, where he took his B.A. degree in approximately 1618.

He first published in 1618, a poem entitled Echo, or the Unfortunate Lovers.

As with many artists of this period full details of his life and career are not recorded. Sources say that after graduating he became "a minister of God's word in or near St Albans." A conversion to the Catholic faith enabled him to become master of St Albans School from 1623–25.

He wrote his first play, Love Tricks, or the School of Complement, which was licensed on February 10th, 1625. From the given date it would seem he wrote this whilst at St Albans but, after its production, he moved to London and to live in Gray's Inn.

For the next two decades, he would write prolifically and with great quality, across a spectrum of thirty plays; through tragedies and comedies to tragicomedies as well as several books of poetry. Unfortunately, his talents were left to wither when Parliament passed the Puritan edict in 1642, forbidding all stage plays and closing the theatres.

Most of his early plays were performed by Queen Henrietta's Men, the acting company for which Shirley was engaged as house dramatist.

Shirley's sympathies lay with the King in battles with Parliament and he received marks of special favor from the Queen.

He made a bitter attack on William Prynne, who had attacked the stage in Histriomastix, and, when in 1634 a special masque was presented at Whitehall by the gentlemen of the Inns of Court as a practical reply to Prynne, Shirley wrote the text—The Triumph of Peace.

Shirley spent the years 1636 to 1640 in Ireland, under the patronage of the Earl of Kildare. Several of his plays were produced by his friend John Ogilby in Dublin in the first ever constructed Irish theatre; The Werburgh Street Theatre. During his years in Dublin he wrote The Doubtful Heir, The Royal Master, The Constant Maid, and St. Patrick for Ireland.

In his absence from London, Queen Henrietta's Men sold off a dozen of his plays to the stationers, who naturally, enough published them. When Shirley returned to London in 1640, he finished with the Queen Henrietta's company and his final plays in London were acted by the King's Men.

On the outbreak of the English Civil War Shirley served with the Earl of Newcastle. However when the King's fortunes began to decline he returned to London. There his friend Thomas Stanley gave him help and thereafter Shirley supported himself in the main by teaching and publishing some educational works under the Commonwealth. In addition to these he published during the period of dramatic eclipse four small volumes of poems and plays, in 1646, 1653, 1655, and 1659.

It is said that he was "a drudge" for John Ogilby in his translations of Homer's Iliad and the Odyssey, and survived into the reign of Charles II, but, though some of his comedies were revived, his days as a playwright were over.

His death, at age seventy, along with that of his wife, in 1666, is described as one of fright and exposure due to the Great Fire of London which had raged through parts of London from September 2nd to the 5th.

He was buried at St Giles in the Fields on October 29th, 1666.

Index of Contents

To the Very Much Honored Walter Moyle, Esq

SIR,

Though the severity of the times took away those dramatique recreations (whose language so much glorified the English Scene) and perhaps looking at some abuses of the common Theaters, which were not so happily purg'd from scurrility, and under-wit, (the onely entertainment of vulgar Capacities) they have outed the more noble and ingenious actions of the eminent stages; The rage yet hath not been Epidemicall, there are left many lovers of this exiled Posie, who are great Masters of reason, and that dare conscientiously own this musical part of Humane learning, when it is presented without the staines of impudence and profanation.

Among these persons, sir you deserve an honorable inscription. For my own part; this is the last which is like to salute the publique view in this kind, and I have onely to say, that I Congratulate my own happiness to conclude with so judicious a Patron.

To make a doubt of your fair receiving this piece: were to dishonor your Character, and make my self undeserving. Read at your leisure, what is humbly presented to your eye and judgment, while I preserve my confidence in your vertue and good thoughts upon

Sir,
The most humble honorer of your worth
JAMES SHIRLEY

DRAMATIS PERSONAE

King of Norway, Easy and credulous in his nature, and passionately doting upon Queen Marpisa.
Gotharus, the politician, active to serve his pleasures and ambition, a great favorite of the Queen.
Turgesius, the Prince, of a gallant disposition, and honoured by the souldier.
Duke Olaus, the Kings Uncle, old, cholerique and distast'd with the Court-proceedings, disaffected to **Gotharus**, and the Queen, but resolute, and faithfull to the Prince.
Haraldus, Son to Marpisa, young, of a sweet and noble disposition, whom Gotharus would form more bold, and ambitious for the greatness he had design'd.
Reginaldus, Aquinas Captaines.
Hormenus, Cortes two honest Courtiers.
Sueno, Helga a couple of Court-Parasites.
Souldiers.
Rebells.
Attendants.
Marpisa the Queen, a 'proud subtle and revengefull Lady, from the widow of Count Altomarus, advanc'd to royall condition, by the practise of her creature and confident, Gotharus.
Albina, wife to Gotharus a vertuous but suffering Lady, under the tyranny of an imperious, and disloyall husband.

SCENE - NORWAY

THE POLITITIAN

A Gallery in the Palace.

Enter **CORTES** and **HORMENUS**.

CORTES
It was a strange and suddaine marriage.

HORMENUS
Could he not love her for the game, and so forth,
But he must thus exalt her? no lesse title
Then Queen, to satisfie her ambition?

CORTES
'Tis a brave rise!

HORMENUS
I did not prophesie,
When the honest Count her husband Altomarus
Liv'd, she would bring us on our knees.

CORTES
I hope
She'l love the King for't.

HORMENUS
And in his absence,
Gotharus the Kings Minion, her old friend,
He has done this royall service; beside, what
Rests on accompts in her old husbands dayes.
I do suspect her Son Haraldus was
Got with more heat, and blood, then Altomarus
Age could assure her, but hee's dead.

CORTES
—Be with him;
Although I wo'not make oath for her chastity,
That boyes good nature is an argument
To me, Gotharus had no share in him:
Hee's honest, of a gentle disposition,
And on my Conscience does pray sometimes.

[Enter **GOTHARUS** reading a Letter.

HORMENUS
No more, we have a Wolfe by'th'eare, what news
From Hell? he cannot want intelligence, he has
So many friends there—he's displeas'd, there is
Some goodness in that Letter, I will pawne
My head, that makes him angry.

[Enter some with Petitions, **GOTHARUS** frowns upon 'em, they returne hastily.

How his frown
Hath scatterrd 'em like leaves, they fly from him
As nimbly, as their bodyes had no more weight
Then their Petitions; I would give an eye-tooth,
To read but three lines.

GOTHARUS
Curse upon his victory!
I meant him not this safety, when I wrought
The King to send him forth to warre, but hop'd
His active spirit would have met some engine
To have translated him to another world;
He's now upon return.

[Exit.

HORMENUS
Would I had but
The harrowing of your skull; my genius gives me
That Paper is some good news of the Prince,
I would I knew it but concern'd him.

CORTES
'Twas
My wonder, the King would send his Son abroad
To warres, the onely pledge of his succession.

HORMENUS
He had a Councellor, this Politition,
That would prefer the Prince to Heaven, a place
His Lordship has no hope to be acquainted with;
The Prince, and his great Uncle Duke Olaus,
Would not allow these pranks of State, nor see
The King betrai'd to a Concubine;
Therefore it was thought fit they should be engag'd
To forraigne dangers.

[Enter **ALBINA**, and her waiting **WOMAN**.

'Tis Madam Albina,
Our great mans wife.

CORTES
The King did seem to affect her,
Before he married her to his favorite.

HORMENUS
Dost think she's honest?

CORTES
Ile not stake my soul on't,
But I believe she is too good for him,
Although the King and she have private conference.

HORMENUS
She looks as she were discontent.

[Exit **ALBINA**

CORTES
She has cause
In being Gotharus wife, some say she lov'd him
Most passionately.

HORMENUS
'Twas her destiny;
She has him now, and if she love him still,
'Tis not impossible she may be a Martyr,
His proud and rugged nature will advance
Her patience too't.

[Enter **HELGA** and **SUENO**.

HELGA
Avoid the Gallery.

SUENO
The King is coming, oh my Lord, your pardon:

HORMENUS
Nay we must all obey.

CORTES
I near lik'd
This fellow.

HORMENUS

He is one of fortunes Minions
The love of the choice Ladyes of the Landry,
That's one that draws in the same team, but more
Inclin'd to'th Knave; he is a kind of Pendant
To the Kings ear, an everlasting parasite:
The King? Albina return'd with him.

[Exit.

[Enter **KING** and **ALBINA**.

KING
Leave us.

[Exit **SUENO** and **HELGA**.

Y'are most unkind to your self in my opinion,
You know well who I am, and what I have
Advanc'd you too; neither in virgin state
Nor marriage, to allow your King a favour?

ALBINA
Sir, let the humble duty of a subject,
Who shall with zealous prayers solicite heaven
For you, and your fair Queen—

KING
Had you been wise,
That might have been your Title, but the God
Of love had with his Arrow so engraven
Gotharus in your heart; you had no language
But what concern'd his praise, scarce any thought
At liberty; I did imagine, when
I had compassion of your sufferings,
And gave thee a fair Bride to my Gotharus,
You would not lose the memory of my benefit,
But (now in state, and nature to reward it)
Consented to returne me love.

ALBINA
Be pleas'd
To excuse the boldnesse of one question.

KING
Be free Albina.

ALBINA
Do not you love my husband?

KING
There wants no testimony, beside the rest,
My giving thee to him, dear to my thoughts,
Is argument I love him.

ALBINA
Would you take
Me back agen? you but betraid his faith,
And your own gift, to tempt me to forsake him.

KING
You are more apprehensive, if you please
He shall possesse you still, I but desire
Sometimes a neere and loving conversation,
Though he should know't, considering how much
I may deserve, he would be wise enough
To love thee near the worse; he's not the first
Lord that hath purchas'd offices by the free
Surrender of his wife to the Kings use,
'Tis frequent in all common-wealths to lend
Their play-fellows to a friend.

ALBINA
Oh do not think
Gotharus can be worth your love, to be
So most degenerate, and lost to honour;
You have a Queen, to whom your vow is sacred,
Be just to her, the blessing is yet warm
Pronounc'd by holy Priest, stain not a passion
To wander from that beauty, richer far
Then Mine; let your souls meet and kiss each other,
That while you live, the examples of chaste love
(Most glorious in a King and Queen) we may
Grow up in vertue by the spring of yours,
Till our top-boughs reach heaven.

KING
You are resolved then
We must be strangers, should my life depend
On the possession of your bosome, I
Should languish and expire, I see.

ALBINA
Good heaven
Will not permit the King want so much goodness,
To think the enjoying of forbidden pleasure
Could benefit his life, rather let mine

Ebbe at some wound, and wander with my blood
By your command ta'ne from me, on my knee—

[Kneels.

KING
Rise, I may kiss Albina—

[Kisses her.

[From behind enters **GOTHARUS**.

GOTHARUS
Ha!

KING
'Thas shot
Another flame into me, come you must—

ALBINA.
What?

KING
Be a woman, do't, or ile complain.
Alb.
To whom?

KING
Thy husband.

GOTHARUS
Horror!

KING
Think upon't.

[Exit.

ALBINA
What will become of miserable Albina?
Like a poor Deere pursu'd to a steep precipice,
That overlooks the Sea, by some fierce hound;
The lust of a wild King doth threaten here,
Before me, the neglects of him I love,
Gotharus my unkind Lord, like the waves,
And full as deafe affright me.

GOTHARUS

How now Madam?
Come, can you kiss?

[Kisses her.

ALBINA
Kiss sir?

GOTHARUS
What difference
Between his touch and mine now? his perhaps
Was with more heat, but mine was soft enough.
What has he promis'd thee, but that's no matter,
Thou wo't be wise enough to make thy bargain,
I father all, onely the King shall give it
A name, he'l make it master of a Province.

ALBINA
What means my Lord:

GOTHARUS
Thou thinkst I am jealous now, not I, I knew
Before he doated on thee, and it is
To be presum'd, having a veile to hide
Thy blushes, (I do mean our marriage)
Thou maist find out some time to meet, and mingle
Stories and limbs, it may be necessary;
And 'cause I will be dutifull to the King,
We will converse no more abed, ile be
Thy husband still Albina, and weare my buds
Under my haire close like a prudent Statesman;
But 'twere not much amisse, as I advis'd
Before, and these new premises consider'd,
You appear abroad with a less train, your Wardrobe
Will make you more suspected, if it be
Too rich; and some whole dayes to keepe your Chamber,
Will make the King know where to find you certain.

ALBINA
Will you have patience my Lord to hear me?

GOTHARUS
The world doth partly think thee honest too,
That will help much, if you observe good rules
And dyet, without tedious progresses,
And visiting of Ladyes, expert in
Night Revels, Masks, and twenty other torments
To an estate; your Doctors must be left too,

I wo'not pay a fee to have your pulse
Felt, and your hand roll'd up like wax, by one
Whose footcloth must attend, while he makes leggs,
And every other morning comes to tell
Your Ladyship a story out of Aretine,
That can set you a longing for diseases,
That he may cure you, and your waiting-woman,
Whose curiosity would taste your Glister,
Commend the operation from her stomack.
Should you be sick, and sick to death, I wo'd
Not counsell you to physick; women are
Fraile things, and should a cordiall miscarry,
My conscience would be arraign'd, and I
Might be suspected for your poisoner.
No, no, I thank you, y'are in a fine course
To ease me wife; or if you must be loose,
I'th spring and fall, let the King bear the charges.
He will, if you apply your selfe.

ALBINA
I am wretched;
Why do you without hearing thus condemn me?
The Lady lives not with a purer faith
To her lov'd Lord, then I have; nor shall greatness,
Nor death it selfe, have power to break it.

[Weeps.

GOTHARUS
Come,
These are but painted teares, leave this, have you
Prepar'd your last accompts?

ALBINA
They are ready sir;
Never was Lady slav'd thus like Albina,
A stipendary, worse, a servile steward,
To give him an accompt of all my expences.

GOTHARUS
I'le have it so in spight of customes heart,
While you are mine; accountless liberty
Is ruine of whole families: now leave me,

[Exit **ALBINA**.

We may talk more anon, I have observ'd
This privacy before, search here Gotharus,

'Tis here from whence mutinous thoughts conspiring
With witty melancholly, shal beget
A strong born mischiefe, I'le admit she be
Honest, I love her not, and if he tempt her
To sinne, that's paid him back in his wives loosness;
From whom I took my first ambition,
And must go on, till we can sway the Kingdom,
Though we clime to't o're many deaths. I first
Practise at home, my unkindness to Albina,
If she do love me must needs break her heart.

[Enter **HARALDUS**.

HARALDUS
My honour'd Lord.

GOTHARUS
Most dear Haraldus welcome,
Preciously welcome to Gotharus heart.

HARALDUS
The Queen my mother, sir, would speake with you.

GOTHARUS
How excellently do those words become thee,
'Tis fit Haraldus Mother be a Queen,
Th'art worth a princely fate; I will attend her.

HARALDUS
Ile tell her so.

GOTHARUS
'Tis not an office for you.

HARALDUS
It is my duty sir, to wait upon
My mother.

GOTHARUS
Who i'th Court is not your servant?
You doe not exercise command enough,
You are too gentle in your fortunes sir,
And weare your greatnesse, as you were not born
To be a Prince.

HARALDUS
My birth sure gave me not
That title, I was born with the condition

To obey, not govern.

GOTHARUS
Do not wrong those Starres,
Which early as you did salute the world,
Design'd this glorious fate; I did consult,
And in the happy minute of thy birth,
Collect what was decreed in heaven about thee.

HARALDUS
Those books are 'bove my reading, but what
E're my stars determine of me, 'tis but late
I heard my mother say, you are on earth,
To whom I am most bound for what I am:

GOTHARUS [aside]
'Tis a shrewd truth, if thou knew'st all.

HARALDUS
You have
Been more a father then a friend to us.

GOTHARUS
Friend to thy Mother, I confess in private,
The other followes by a consequence, [aside].
A father my Haraldus? I confess
I was from thy nativity inclin'd
By a most strange and secret force of nature,
Or sympathy to love thee like my owne;
And let me tell thee, though thy mother had
Merit enough to engage my senses;
Yet there was something more in thee consider'd,
That rais'd my thoughts, and study to advance
Thee to these pregnant hopes of state, methinks
I see thee a King already.

HARALDUS
Good sir, do not
Prompt me to that ambition, I possess
Too much already, and I could, so pleas'd
My Mother, travell where I should not hear
Of these great titles, and it comes now aptly,
I should entreat your Lordshp to assist me
In a request to her, I know she loves you,
And will deny you nothing; I would faine
Visit the University for study,
I do lose time methinks.

GOTHARUS
Fie Haraldus,
And leave the Court? how you forget your selfe?
Study to be King,
I shall halfe repent my care,
If you permit these dull and phlegmatick
Thoughts to usurpe, they'l stifle your whole reason,
Catch at the Sunne, devest him of his beame,
And in your eye wear his proud rayes; let day
Be when you smile, and when your anger points,
Shoot death in every frowne: covet a shade,
Affect a solitude, and books, and forfeit,
So brave an expectation?

HARALDUS
Of what?

GOTHARUS
Of Norwayes Crown.

HARALDUS
Could there be any thought
Within me so ambitious, with what hope
Could it be cherished, when I have no title?

GOTHARUS
I that have thus farre studied thy fortune,
May find a way.

HARALDUS
The King —

GOTHARUS
Is not immortal while he has Physitians.

HARALDUS
What's that vnsaid? The King is happy,
And the whole Nation treasure up their hopes
In Prince Turgesius, who with his great uncle
Valiant Olaus.

GOTHARUS
Are sent to'th warres, where 'twill concerne 'm,
To think of fame, and how to march to honour
Through death.

HARALDUS [aside]
I dare not hear him.

GOTHARUS
Or if they
Return—

HARALDUS
They will be welcome to all good
Mens hearts, and next the King, none with more joy
Congratulate their safeties, then your selfe:
I am confident my Lord you will remember
To see my Mother, and excuse me if
To finish something else I had in charge,
I take my leave, all good dwell with your Lordship.

[Exit.

GOTHARUS
But that I have Marpisas faith, I could
Suspect him not the issue of my blood,
He is too tame, and honest, at his yeers
I was prodigiously in love with greatnesse;
Or if not mine, let him inherit but
His Mothers soule, she has pride enough, and spirit
To catch at flames, his education
Has been too soft, I must new form the boy
Into more vice, and daring, strange, we must
Study at Court, how to corrupt our Children.

[Enter **QUEEN MARPISA**.

The Queen!

QUEEN MARPISA
My expectation to speak
With thee Gotharus, was too painfull to me;
I feare we are all undone; dost hear the news?
The Prince is comming back with victory,
Our day will be o're-cast.

GOTHARUS
These eyes will force
A brighter from those clouds; are not you Queen?

QUEEN MARPISA
But how Turgesius, and his bold uncle
Wil look upon me.

GOTHARUS

Let 'em stare out
Their eyeballs, be you mistress still of the
Kings heart, and let their gall spout in their stomack,
We'l be secure.

QUEEN MARPISA
Thou art my fate.

GOTHARUS
I must confesse
I was troubled when I heard it first; seem not
You pale at their return, but put on smiles
To grace their triumph; now you have most need
Of womans art, dissemble cunningly.

QUEEN MARPISA
My best Gotharus.

GOTHARUS
They shall find stratagems in peace, more fatal
Then all the Engines of the war; what mischiefe
Will not Gotharus fly to, to assure
The fair Marpisa's greatness, and his own,
In being hers (an Empire 'bove the world)
There is a heaven in either eye, that calls
My adoration, such Promethean fire,
As were I struck dead in my works, shouldst thou
But dart one look upon me, it would quicken
My cold dust, and informe it with a soul
More daring then the first.

QUEEN MARPISA
Still my resolv'd Gotharus.

GOTHARUS
Let weak Statesmen think of conscience,
I am arm'd against a thousand stings, and laugh at
The tales of Hell, and other worlds, we must
Possess our joyes in this, and know no other
But what our fancy every minute shall
Create to please us.

QUEEN MARPISA
This is harmony,
How dull is the Kings language, I could dwell
Upon thy lips; why should not we engender
At every sense?

GOTHARUS
Now you put me in mind,
The pledge of both our hopes, and blood, Haraldus,
Is not well bred, he talks too morally,
He must have other discipline, and be fashion'd
For our great aims upon him; a Crown never
Became a Stoick, pray let me commend
Some conversation to his youth.

QUEEN MARPISA
He is thine.

[Enter **HELGA**.

GOTHARUS
He shall be every way my own.

HELGA
The King desires your presence Madam.

QUEEN MARPISA
I attend, you'l follow —

[Exit.

GOTHARUS
Thee to death, and triumph in
My ruines for thy sake, a thousand forms
Throng in my braine, that is the best, which speeds,
Who looks at Crowns, must have no thought who bleeds.

[Exit.

ACT II

SCENE I

An Apartment in the Palace.

Enter **KING, HORMENUS, CORTES, SUENO**.

KING
This musick doth but add to melancholly,
Ile hear no more.

CORTES

He's strangely mov'd.

HORMENUS
I cannot think a cause,
You were wont to fool him into mirth; Where's Helga
Your dear companion? no device between you
To raise his thoughts?

SUENO
I am nothing without my fellow,
Musick is best in Consort.

HORMENUS
Your buffonry is musical belike.

CORTES
Your Juglers cannot do some o'their tricks
Without confederacy.

SUENO
I'le try alone.
If please your Majesty there is—

KING
That—

[Strikes him.

For your unseasonable and saucie fooling.

HORMENUS
That was a musical box o'th' ear.

KING
Leave us.

CORTES
'Tis nothing without a fellow, he knows
Musick is best in Consort.

[Exit.

SUENO
Would you had your parts?

[Exit.

KING

Hormenus you may stay.

HORMENUS
Your pleasure sir.

KING
Men do account thee honest.

HORMENUS [aside]
'Tis possible
I May fare the worse.

KING
And wise; canst tell the cause why I am sad?

HORMENUS
Not I sir.

KING
Nor I my self, 'tis strange I should be subject
To a dull passion, and no reason for it.

HORMENUS
These things are frequent.

KING
Sometimes ominous,
And do portend.

HORMENUS
If you enjoy a health,
What is in fate?

KING
I am King
Still, and I not?

HORMENUS
We are all happy in't,
And when time shall with the consent of nature,
Call you an old man from this world to heaven,
May he that shall suceed you, Prince Turgesius,
The glory of our hope, be no less fortunate.

KING
My Son,
I was too rash to part with him.

HORMENUS
We should
Have thought his stay a blessing, and did wish
You would not have expos'd such tender years
To the rough warre; but your commands met with
His duty, and our obedience.

KING
It is very
Strange, we of late hear no success, I hope
This sadnesse is not for his loss, he has
A kinsman with him, loves him dearly, 'tis
The Queen.

[Enter **QUEEN MARPISA** and **HELGA**.

I feel my drooping thoughts fall off,
And my clouds fly before the wind, her presence
Hath an infusion to restore dead nature.
My sweet, my dear Marpisa.

QUEEN MARPISA
You sent for me.

KING
I am but the shadow of my selfe without thee.

[Enter **CORTES, SUENO**.

No wonder I was sad, my soul had plac'd
All her delight in these fair eyes, and could not
But think it selfe an exile in thy absence,
Why should we ever part, but chaine our selves
Together thus?

SUENO
He's in a better humour I hope;
I do not think but his Majestie would cuffe well,
His hand carryes a princely weight.

HELGA
A favour.

SUENO
Would you might weare such another in your eare.

KING
Come hither—on this side.

SUENO

You were on that side before.

KING

Wo'dst not thou lose thy life, to do a service
My Queen would smile upon?

SUENO

Alas, My life
Is the least thing to be imagin'd, he
Is not a faithful subject would refuse
To kill his wife and children, after that
To hang himselfe, to do the Queen a service.

KING

Come hither, Helga.

HELGA

Royal sir.

KING

What would affright thy undertaking, to deserve
The least grace from my Queen?

HELGA

I cannot tell,
But I've an opinion, the Devill could not;
My life is nothing fir, to obtaine her favour,
I would hazard more; I have heard talk of hell,
So farre she should command me.

HORMENUS

Bless me goodness!
What wretched Parasites are these? how can
The King be patient at 'em? here is flattery
So thick and grosse, it would endure a hand-saw.

CORTES

His judgement's I fear stupified.

HORMENUS

Come hither,
Which of you can resolve, what serpent spawn'd you?

SUENO

You are pleasant.

HELGA
My good Lord, it hurts not you,
There is necessity of some knaves, and so
Your Lordship be exempted, why should you
Trouble your selfe, and murmur at our courses?

[Enter **AQUINUS** hastily.

AQUINUS
The King!

HELGA
Peace.

SUENO
Your businesse?

AQUINUS
News from the field!

SUENO
Good?

AQUINUS
Good.

HELGA
How?

SUENO
How prethee?

AQUINUS
The day, the field, the safety, O the glory
Of warre is Norwaies, Letters to the King!—

HELGA
Give 'em to me.

SUENO
Or me.

HELGA
Trust not a fool with things of consequence,
He's the Kings mirth, let me present the news.

SUENO
Sir, I should know you; this is a knave,

Would take to him all the glory of your report;
If please you, let me present the Letters.

HELGA
My Leige!

SUENO
My Soveraigne!

HELGA
News!

SUENO
Good news!

HELGA
Excellent newes!

SUENO
The Prince?

HELGA
The Prince is—

SUENO
The enemy is—o'rethrown.

HELGA
They have lost the day.

SUENO
Defeated utterly.

HELGA
And are all slain.

SUENO
Madam, will you hear the news?

KING
Say on, what is't you would relate?

HELGA
One of my creatures sir hath brought you Letters,

[**AQUINUS** delivers the Letters.

My servant sir, one strengthened to your service

Out of my maintenance, an instrument of mine,
So please you to consider my duty in his service.

AQUINUS
Why hark you Gentlemen, I have but mock'd
Your greedy zeals, there's no such matter in
Those Letters as you have told; we have lost all,
And the Prince taken prisoner, will you not
Stay for the reward, you know I'm but your Creature,
I look for nothing but your courtly faces
To pay my travel.

HELGA
We wo'not appear yet—

[Exit.

AQUINUS
How the Rats vanish.

KING
Read here my best Marpisa, news that makes
A triumph in my heart, great as the conquest
Upon our enemies; Hormenus, Cortes,
Our Son will prove a Souldier, was my sadnesse
Omen to this good fate? or nature fear'd
The extasie of my joy would else o'recome me?
They are return'd victorious.

HORMENUS
Thanks to heaven!

KING
And some reward is due to thee; wear that
For the Kings sake.

[Gives him a ring.

AQUINUS
You too much honour me.

KING
But something in Marpisa's face, shews not
So clear a joy as we express, forbear,

[Exeunt **CORTES**, **HORMENUS** and **AQUINUS**.

Wait till we call; can this offend my Queen,

To hear of happinesse to my Son? O let
Thy eyes look bright, there shine hath force to make
The wreath of Laurel grow upon his temples;
Why dost thou weep? this dew will kill the victory,
And turn his Bay to Cipresse.

QUEEN MARPISA
Witnesse heaven,
There's not a teare that mourns for him, his safety
And conquest is most welcome, and he shall
Have still my prayers, he may grow up in fame,
And all the glorious fortunes of a Prince:
But while my wishes fly to heaven for blessings
Upon his head, at the same time, I must
Remember in what miserable condition
My stars have plac'd me.

KING
What can make thy state
Guilty of such a name, and so deject
Thy nobler thoughts? am not I still the King?
And is not fair Marpisa mine by marriage?
Crown'd here my Queen immortally.

QUEEN MARPISA
Though I be
By royall bounty of your love, possest
Of that great Title sir, I have some fears.

KING
You amaze me, speak thy doubts at large.

QUEEN MARPISA
The Prince
(Dear to your love, and I still wish him so)
(Dear to your peoples hearts) I fear, will think
Our marriage his dishonour, and Olaus
Your passionate Uncle, no good friend of mine,
When he shall see to what a height your love
And holy vow hath rais'd me, most unworthy,
Will but salute Marpisa with his scorn,
And by his counsell, or some waies of force
Unchain our hearts, and throw me from your bosome
To death, or worse, to shame; oh think upon me,
And if you have one fear that's kin to mine,
Prevent their tyrannie, and give me doom
Of exile e're their cruelty arrive:
Ile take my sentence kindly from your lips,

Though it be killing.

KING
Let my Son or Uncle,
Dare but affront three in a look, I shall
Forget the ties of nature, and discharge 'em
Like the corruption in my blood.

QUEEN MARPISA
I can
Submit my selfe to them, and would you please
To allow my humblenesse no staine to what
You have advanc'd me to, I can be their servant,
And with as true a duty wait upon 'em—

KING
Thou art all goodnesse, twenty Kingdoms are
Too little for thy dowry; who attends?

[Enter **HORMENUS** and **CORTES** and **AQUINUS**.

Thus every minute I will marry thee,
And wear thee in my heart.

[Kisses her.

—Vanish the thought
Of all thy sex beside, and what can else
Attempt our separation: th'art obscure,
And liv'st in Court but like a maskquing star,
Shut from us by the unkindnesse of a cloud
When Cynthia goes to Revels: I will have
A chariot for my Queen richer then er'e
Was shewn in Roman triumph, and thou shalt
Be drawn with Horses white as Venus doves,
Till heaven it selfe in envy of our bliss,
Snatch thee from earth to place thee in his Orbe,
The brightest constellation.

CORTES
He dotes strangely.

KING
Hormenus, Cortes, I would have you all
Search your inventions to advance new joyes;
Proclaime all pleasures free, and while my fair
Queen smiles, it shall be death for any man
I'th Court to frown.

[Exeunt **KING** and **QUEEN MARPISA**.

HORMENUS
You ha' not so much love i'th Court Aqninus.

CORTES
How do you like the Queen?

AQUINUS
Why she's not married,
He does but call her so.

HORMENUS
And lyes with her.

AQUINUS
The Prince yet knows it not.

HORMENUS
He'l meet it coming home.

[Enter **GOTHARUS**.

GOTHARUS
Aquinus?

[Takes **AQUINUS** aside.

AQUINUS
Sir.

GOTHARUS
You brought Letters from the Camp.

AQUINUS
I did my Lord.

HORMENUS
What in the name of Policy is now hatching?
I do not like those fawning postures in him,
How kind they are.

GOTHARUS
That Souldier is thought honest.

HORMENUS
But if he cringe once more I shall suspect him,

That leg confirms he is corrupt already.

GOTHARUS
How does he like his fathers marriage?

AQUINUS
We had no fame on't there when I set forth.

GOTHARUS
'T was strange and suddain, but we are all happy
In the good Princes health and victory;
The Duke Olaus too I hope is well.

AQUINUS
He was design'd at my departure,
To be here before the Army.

GOTHARUS
He will be welcome:
You shall accept the price of a new Armour,
And wherein any power of mine can serve you
I'th Court, command.

AQUINUS
I am your Lord-ships creature.

[Exeunt.

HORMENUS
They are gone, I long to see the Prince
How do you think his Highnesse will
Behave himself to his new mother Queen?
Will it be treason not to aske her blessing?

CORTES
I am confident his Uncle, brave Olaus.

[Enter **HARALDUS**.

Wo'not run mad for joy of the Kings marriage?

HORMENUS
Let them look to't, there may be alterations.

HARALDUS
They talk sure of my mother and the King.

HORMENUS

Secure as they account themselves, the Prince
Must be receiv'd spight of Marpisa's greatnesse,
And all the tricks of her incarnate fiend
Gotharus, who both plot I fear, to raise
That Composition of their blood,
Haraldus—

HARALDUS
How was that?

HORMENUS
The strange effect
Of their luxurious appetites, though in him
Poor innocence, suspecting not their sin,
We read no such ambition.

HARALDUS
Oh my shame!
What have my ears receiv'd? am I a bastard?
'Tis malice that doth wound my Mothers honour;
How many bleed at once? yet now I call
To memory, Gotharus at our loving
Late conference, did much insult upon
The name of a Father, and his care of me
By some strange force of nature: ha! my fears
Shoot an Ice through me, I must know the truth
Although it kill me.

[Exit.

CORTES
Who was that Haraldus?

HORMENUS
I hope he did not hear us, again Gotharus.
And the two squirrels; more devices yet.

[Enter **GOTHARUS, SUENO**, and **HELGA**.

SUENO
Let us alone my Lord, we'l quicken him.

GOTHARUS
You must use all your art to win him to't.

HELGA
Let us alone to make him drink, we are the credit
Of the Court for that, he's but a child alas, we'l take our time.

[Enter **OLAUS** attended with **CAPTAINS**.

OLAUS
Hormenus.

HORMENUS
My good Lord Olaus, I
Joy in your safe return, how fares the Prince?

OLAUS
Well, where's the King?

HORMENUS
Kissing his new made Queen Marpisa.

OLAUS
Ha!
The King is married then.

GOTHARUS
Away!

The Duke Olaus! sir—

[Exit **SUENO** & **HORMENUS**

OLAUS
I am too stiffe for Complement,
My Lord, I have rid hard—

[Exit.

GOTHARUS
He has met the intelligence,
And is displeas'd with me the state of things at home;
This marriage stings him, let it, we must have
No trembling hearts, not fall into an ague,
Like Children at the sight of a portent:
But like a Rock when wind and waves go highest,
And the insulting billowes dash against
Her ribs, be unmov'd. The King must be saluted
With other Letters, which must counterfet
The Princes character, I was his Secretary
And know the Art, malice inspire my brain
To poyson his opinion of his Son;
Ile form it cunningly.
Ha! 'tis Haraldus.

[Enter **HARALDUS**.

He looks sad.

HARALDUS
I dare not aske
My mother, 'twere a crime, but one degree
Beneath the sinfull act that gave me life
To question her, and yet to have this fright
Dwell in my apprehension, without
The knowledge of some truth, must needs distract
My poor wits quite; 'tis he, I will take boldnesse
And know the worst of him, If I be what
I am already charactred, he can
Resolved my shame too well.

GOTHARUS
How is't my Lord?

HARALDUS
Never so ill sir.

GOTHARUS
Art sick?

HARALDUS
Most dangerously.

GOTHARUS
Where?

HARALDUS
Here, at heart, which bleeds with such a wound,
As none but you, can cure.

GOTHARUS
Ile drop my soul
Into it, shew me how I may
Be thy Physitian, to restore thy blood
I will lose all mine, speak child.

HARALDUS
This very love
Is a fresh suffering, and your readinesse
To cure my sorrow, is another wound;
You are too kind, why are you so? what is
Or can be thought in me fit to deserve it?

GOTHARUS

Thou dost talk wildly; to accuse me thus
For loving thee, could the world tempt me here,
And court me with her glories to forsake thee,
Thus I would dwell about thy neck, and not
Be bought from kissing thee for all her provinces:
There is a charme upon my soul to love thee,
And I must do't.

HARALDUS

Then I must dye.

GOTHARUS

Forbid it gentler fates.

HARALDUS

If I could hear you wish
Me dead, I should have hope to live; although
I would not willingly deserve your anger,
By any impious deed, you do not know
What comfort it would be to heare you curse me.

GOTHARUS

He's mad; Haraldus, prethee do not talk so.

HARALDUS

Or if you think a curse too much to help me,
Yet rail upon me, but do't heartily, and call me

GOTHARUS

What?

HARALDUS

Vilaine, or Bastard, sir,
The worst is best from you.

GOTHARUS

Thou dost amaze me.

HARALDUS

Will you not for me?
Then for my mothers sake if you do love her,
Or ever did esteem her worth your friendship,
Let me entreat you draw your sword, and give me
Something to wear in blood upom my bosome;
Write but one letter of your name upon
My brest, Ile call you father, by your love;

Do something that may make me bleed a little.

GOTHARUS
By that I dare not, thou hast nam'd Haraldus
A father.

HARALDUS
I but call you so, I know
You are a stranger to my blood, although
Indeed to me your great affection
Appears a wonder; nor can nature shew
More in a Parent to a child; but if
I be.

GOTHARUS
What?

HARALDUS
I shall blush sir to pronounce it,
There's something that concerns my mother, will not
Give it a name; yet I would be resolv'd,
That I might place my duty right; If I
Must answer to your Sonne, you may imagine
I shall no more aske you a reason, why
You have been so kind to me; and to my mother.

GOTHARUS
Thou hast said it, th'art mine own, 'twas nature in me,
That could not hide the actions of a Father.

HARALDUS
I am your base seed then.

GOTHARUS
Stain not thy self
With such a name, but look upon thy mother
Now made a Queen.

HARALDUS
You made her first a strumpet,
And it would aske the piety of her Sonne,
To dye upon that man that stole her honour:
Why did you so undo us? why did you
Betray my mother to this shame? or when
She had consented, why should both your lust
Curse my unsinning heart, oh I must be
For your vice scorn'd, though innocent.

GOTHARUS

None dare—

HARALDUS

I should not by your vertue have been sav'd,
Where shall I hide my life, I must no more
Converse with men—

GOTHARUS

Thou art too passionate.

HARALDUS

I will entreat my mother we may go
Into some wildernesse, where we may find
Some Creatures that are spotted like our selves,
And live and dye there, be companion
To the wild Panther, and the Leopard, yet
They are too good for their converse, we are
By ours, defil'd, their spots do make them fair.

[Exit.

GOTHARUS

'Tis time that Sueno and his companion,
Dispers'd these clouds; now to the King, with whom
If the Queens beauty keep her magick, then
Our Engine mount, and day grows bright agen.

[Exeunt.

ACT III

SCENE I

An Apartment in the Palace.

Enter **KING, QUEEN MARPISA, OLAUS, REGINALDUS, AQUINUS, HELGA**.

KING

Uncle, I am glad to see you.

OLAUS

I am not glad
To see you sir.

KING

Not me?

OLAUS
Consorted thus.

KING
If Olaus be forgetfull of good manners,
I shall forget his years, and blood; be temperate.

OLAUS
There's something in your blood that will undoe
Your state and fame eternally, purge that,
You know I never flatter'd you, that woman
Will prove thy evill Genius.

KING
Y'are too saucy.

OLAUS
Do not I know her, was she not wife
To the Count Altomarus a weak Lord?
But too good for her, charm'd by the flattery
And magick of her face, and tongue, to dote
And Marry her, born of a private Family,
Advanc'd thus, she grew insolent, and I fear
By pride and liberty, and some trick she had,
Broke her good husbands heart.

QUEEN MARPISA
Sir, you much wrong me,
And now exceed the priviledge of your birth
To injure mine.

OLAUS
We all know you can plead
Your own defence, you have a womans wit,
Heaven send you equall modesty, I am plain.

QUEEN MARPISA
It would be held an insolence in others,
And saucy boldnesse in the sacred presence
Thus of the King, to accuse, whom he hath pleas'd
To take companion of his bed; and though
It would become the justice of my cause
And honour, to desire these black aspersions
May be examin'd further, and the Author
Call'd to make proof of such a passionate language,
(Which will betray his accusation was

But envy of my fortunes) I remember
Y'are the Kings Uncle, and 'tis possible
You may be abus'd by some malicious tale
Fram'd to dishonour me, and therefore I
Beseech you humbly sir, to let this passe
But as an act in him of honest freedom,
Beside what else may give you priviledge
Being a Souldier, and not us'd to file
His language, blunt and rugged wayes of speech
Becoming your profession.

OLAUS
Very good!
Although we ha' not the device of tongue
And soft phrase Madam, which you make an Idol
At Court, and use it to disguise your heart,
We can speak truth in our unpollish'd words,
Thou art—

QUEEN MARPISA
What am I?

OLAUS
Not the Queen.

KING
She is
My wife Olaus.

OLAUS
I must never kneel to her,
Nor the good Prince your son, the hope of war,
And peaces darling, honour of our blood,
And worth a better Kingdom then he's born to—

KING
What of him?

OLAUS
Must never call her Mother.

KING
Dare you instruct him
Against his duty, leave us.

OLAUS
You have lost
More honour in those minutes you were married,

Then we have gain'd in months abroad, with all
Our triumph purchas'd for you with our blood;
Is this the payment, the reward for all
Our faith? when thy young Son, whose springing valour
And name, already makes the confines tremble,
Returns like young Augustus crown'd with victories;
Must a stepdame first salute him,
And tread upon his Laurel?

KING
Leave the Court.

OLAUS
May it not prove an Hospital! 'tis i'th way
To change a title, lust and all the riots
Of licence reeling in it, by th'example
Of one should least prophane it, I am still
O laus, and your fathers brother.

AQUINUS
My Lord.

KING
Take heed
You do not talk your head off, we have Scaffolds,
But the old man raves, come my Marpisa.

OLAUS
Then I will talke, threaten my head,
Command that Parasite that dares do most
In wickednesse, to shew himselfe your servant;
Give him his engine, and his fee for hangman,
Let him take boldness but to move one hair
That withers on my head out of his posture,
He shall have more hope to o'recome the Devil
In single duel, then to scape my fury.

AQUINUS
Sir—

KING
Our guard.

OLAUS
Look you, i'le bring no danger to your person,
I love you too well; I did alwayes use
To speak, your father lik'd me near the worse.
And now I am coole againe—

You say you are married—

KING
We are.

OLAUS
Then between you, and I, and let none heare us,
To make your selfe, your Son, and Kingdome prosper,
Be counsel'd to a divorce.

KING
Not, not
To save thy soule, my sonnes life added
To thine, and lives of all the Army shall
Be divorc'd from this world first, you are my fathers
Brother, and if you love my sonne, your pupil,
So hopeful in your thoughts, teach him to come
More humbly to us, without thought to question
Our marriage, or i'le find a chastisement
For his rebellious heart, we will.

[Exit.

OLAUS
You must not; I wo'not leave him yet.

[Exit.

REGINALDUS
This freedome may engage his life to danger,
He is too passionate.

AQUINUS
He has said too much,
Ile venter speaking to him.

[Exit.

HELGA
He's alone, now to him.

SUENO
Noble sir— I have a suit to you.

REGINALDUS
A Courtier aske a suit of a Souldier?
You'l wear no Buffe nor Iron?

SUENO

I come very impudently, and I hope to thrive
The better for't; this Gentleman my friend,
A man of quality, and in some grace with
The King, hath laid a wager with me of
Two hundred Crowns, I dare not pull a haire
From your most reverend Beard: now if you please
To give me leave, i'le win the Crownes, laugh at him,
And drink your health at supper.

REGINALDUS

A hair from my beard?

SUENO

But one hair, if shall please you.

REGINALDUS

Come, take it.

SUENO

I have pul'd three noble sir.

REGINALDUS

'Twas more then your commssion, there's one,

[Kicks him.

That's another, and that will make you an upright Courtier.

[Strikes him.

HORMENUS

Ha! Ha!

SUENO

Sir, I beseech you—

REGINALDUS

Beg modestly hereafter, take within your bounds,
You have small beard to play upon. 'tis fit
My fist should make an answer to your wit.

[Exit.

SUENO

I have it to a hair, the cholerick Duke agen?
I am gone.

[Exeunt.

[Enter **OLAUS** & **AQUINUS**.

AQUINUS
Sir, you have been too blame.

OLAUS
How dare you talk to me sir?

AQUINUS
'Tis my duty, and I must tell you,
Y'ave built too much upon him as a kinsman,
And have forgot the King.

OLAUS
Take that for your impudence.

[Strikes him with his Cane.

AQUINUS
I have it, and I thank you.

[Exit.

[Enter **KING**, reading of Letters and **QUEEN MARPISA**, followed by **SUENO**.

HORMENUS
They are gone sir, but have left Prints of their fury,
The angry Duke has broke Aquinus head,
For speaking dutifully on your behalfe;
To'ther mute man of war stroke Sueno sir.

SUENO
I heare his language humming in my head still.

KING
Aquinus? strike so near our presence?

SUENO
Nay these Souldiers will strike a man, if he doe not
Carry himselfe to a hairs breadth, I know that.

KING
They shall repent this impudence, look up
My dear Marpisa, there's no tempest shall
Approach to hurt thee, they have rais'd a storm
To their own ruines.

[Enter a **SOLDIER**.

SUENO
Sir, if you'l bring me
To'th King. you shall do an office worth your labour,
I have Letters will be welcome.

HELGA
You must give
Me leave sir to present 'em from the Prince:
Most excellent, sir, my Soveraigne.

SUENO
Letters? If you have a chaine of gold—

HELGA
Go hang thy selfe.

[**SOULDIER** gives **HELGA** the Letters, & exits.

HELGA
I am most fortunate to present you sir
With Letters from the Prince, and if your Majestie
Knew with what zeale I tender these.

[The **KING** reads.

KING
Ha!

HELGA
He frowns, where's the Soldade? you'l goe my half.

KING
Who brought these Letters? where's the messenger

HORMENUS
He was here but now, he's vanish'd.

KING
Vanish thee too, and creep into the earth.

HORMENUS
I shall sir.

KING
The impudence of Children, read Marpisa,

More Letters from the proud ambitious boy,
He dares to give us precepts, and writes here,
We have too much forgot our selfe and honour,
In making thee our Queen, puts on his grace
A discontent, and sayes, the triumph he
Expected, the reward of his young merit,
Will be ungloried in our suddaine match,
And weak election.

QUEEN MARPISA
This was my fear.

KING
He threatens us, if we proceed with his
Command and power i'th Army; raise new Forces
To oppose 'm, and proclaime 'm Rebels, Trayters—

QUEEN MARPISA
Sir, I beseech you for the generall good,
Temper your rage, these are but words of passion,
The Prince will soon be sorry for't, suspect not
His duty, rather then disgrace your Son,
Divide me from your heart, the people love him.

KING
I'le hate him for't, Gotharus; where's Gotharus,

[Exit.

QUEEN MARPISA
This Letter tast's of his invention,
He's active, it concerns us both. Albina.

[Enter **ALBINA**.

Nay, you may forward Madam.

ALBINA
I beseech
Your pardon, I did hope to have found my Lord
Gotharus here.

QUEEN MARPISA
The King ask'd for him,
And is but new retyr'd, who I presume
If he had known of your approach, w'od not
Have gone so soon.

ALBINA
I have no businesse Madam
With the King.

QUEEN MARPISA
Come do not disguise it thus,
I am covetous to know your suit;
But I am confident he will deny
You nothing, and your husband is of my
Opinion lately.

ALBINA
By your goodnesse Madam,
Let me not suffer in your thoughts, I see
There is some poison thrown upon my innocence,
And tis not well done of my Lord Gotharus,
To render me to your suspition
So unhappy, 'tis too much he has withdrawn
His own heart, he will shew no seeds of charity,
To make all others scorn me.

QUEEN MARPISA
If he do,
You can return it, but take heed your wayes
Be straite to your revenge, let not my fame
And honour be concern'd with the least wound.

ALBINA
I understand not what you mean.

QUEEN MARPISA
I cannot
Be patient, to hear the King commend
Your lip.

ALBINA
I am betray'd.

QUEEN MARPISA
My phrase is modest,
Do not you love the King?

ALBINA
Yes, with the duty—

QUEEN MARPISA
Of one that wants no cunning to dissemble
Her pride, and loose desires.

ALBINA

You are the Queen.

QUEEN MARPISA

What then?

ALBINA

I should else tell you, 'tis ill done
To oppresse one that groans beneath the weight
Of griefe already, and I durst take boldnesse
To say, you were unjust.

QUEEN MARPISA

So, so.

ALBINA

I can
Contain no longer, take from my sad heart
What hitherto I have conceal'd, (in that
You may call me dissembler of my sorrows)
I am weary of my life, and fear not what
Your power and rage can execute; would you
Had no more guilt upon your blood, then I
Have sinne in my accounts that way, My Lord
Gotharus would not be so unkind to me.

QUEEN MARPISA

What's that you said so impudently Albina?

ALBINA

What I did think should have consum'd me here
In silence, but your injuries are mighty,
And though I do expect to have my name
In your black Register design'd for death,
To which my husband will I know consent;
I cannot thus provok'd, but speak what wounds me.
Yet here agen I shut the Casket up,
Never to let this secret forth, to spread
So wide a shame hereafter.

QUEEN MARPISA

Thou hast wak'd
A Lyonness.

ALBINA

Death cannot more undo me,
And since I live an exile from my husband,

I will not doubt but you may soon prevaile,
To give my weary soul a full discharge
Some way or other; and i'th minute when
It takes her flight to an eternall dwelling,
I will forgive you both, and pray for you,
But let not your revenge be to long idle,
Least the unmeasur'd pile of my affections
Weigh me to death before your anger comes,
And so you lose the triumph of your envies.

QUEEN MARPISA
You sha'not be forgotten, feare it not,
And but that something nearer doth concern us,
You should soon find a punishment. The King.

[Exit followed by **ALBINA**.

SCENE II

Another Apartment in the Same.

[Enter **KING, GOTHARUS**, with a Letter.

KING
He struck Aquinus, Helga saw him bleed.

GOTHARUS
These are strange insolencies, one goe for Aquinus.
Did Olaus bring these Letters?

KING
No, some spirit,
For he soon vanish'd.
I have given my sonne
To the most violent men under the Planets,
These Souldiers.

GOTHARUS
And they'l cling to him like Ivie,
Embrace him even to death.

KING
Like Brees to Cattel
In summer, they'l not let him feed.

GOTHARUS

But make
Him fling, unquiet.

KING
Most repineful, spleeny.

GOTHARUS
Ready to break the twist of his Allegiance.

KING
Which they fret every day—

GOTHARUS
These put upon his young blood discontents.

KING
Dangerous—

GOTHARUS
Extremely dangerous.

KING
Swell him up
With the alluring shapes of rule, and Empire—

GOTHARUS
And speak his strength with a proud Emphasis;
Yours, with a faint cold-hearted voice; was ever
Such peremptory lines writ to a father?

KING
Thy counsell, while the dangers yet aloofe.

GOTHARUS
Aloofe? take heed, hils in a piece of landskip
May seem to stand a hundred leagues, yet measure,
There's but an inch in distance; oh ambition
Is a most cunning, infinite dissembler,
But quick i'th execution.

KING
Thy counsell.

GOTHARUS
He that aspires hath no Religion,
He knows no kindred.

KING

I aske for thy advice.

GOTHARUS
Have you not seen a great Oke cleft asunder,
With a small wedge cut from the very heart
Of the same tree?

KING
It frights me to apply it;
Oh my mis-fortune, this is torment, not
A cure.

[Enter **AQUINUS**

GOTHARUS
Aquinus, Speak him gently sir,
And leave me to encourage him in a service
Worth his attempt, and needful to your safety.
Noble Aquinus, our good King has sence
Of the affront you suffered from his Uncle,
And as he is inform'd, for speaking but
The duty of a subject.

AQUINUS
This is true sir,
I wear his bloody favour still, I never
Took any blow so long on trust.

KING
I know thy spirit's daring, and it shal become
My justice to reward thy suffering;
A storm now hovers o're my Kingdom,
When the aire is clear, and our sky fair agen,
Expect, nay challenge, we shall recompence
What thou hast suffer'd for us, with a bounty
Worth all thy merits, i'th mean time apply
Thy selfe to my Gotharus, and be counsel'd.

[Exit.

ALBINA
My duty.

GOTHARUS
Th'hast no alliance to my blood;
Yet if thou think'st I do not flatter thee,
I feel a friendly touch of thy dishonour,
The blow, 'twas not well done of Duke Olaus.

AQUINUS

You great men think you may do what you please,
And if y'have a mind to pound us in a morter
We must obey.

GOTHARUS

That law is none of natures,
And this distinction of birth and royalty
Is not so firme a proofe, but there are men
Have swords to pierce it through, and make the hearts
Of those that take this priviledge from their blood,
Repent they were injurious.

AQUINUS

My sword
Was quiet when he beat me.

GOTHARUS

He did not, could not beat thee.

ALBINA

'Twas worse, he cudgel'd me, I feel it yet,
Nor durst I strike agen.

GOTHARUS

It could not be
A tamenesse in thy spirit, but quick thought
That 'twas Olaus, not, that in thy heart
There was no will to be reveng'd, for he
Is false to nature, loves his injury,
But that there was no safety to return
Thy anger on his person.

AQUINUS

Y'are i'th right,
That frighted me.

GOTHARUS

For he is not reveng'd,
That kills his enemy and destroyes himselfe,
For doing his own justice, therefore men
That are not slaves, but free, these we receive
Born, and bred Gentlemen in fair employments,
That have, and dare bid high agen for honour,
When they are wrong'd by men 'bove them in title,
As they are thought worthy a personall wound,
In that are rais'd and level'd with the injurer;

And he that shall provoke me with his weapon,
By making me his enemy, makes me equal,
And on those terms I kill him: But there is
Another caution to wise men, who ought
To cast and make themselves secure, that when
They have return'd full payment for their sufferings
In fame, they may be safe without a guard.

AQUINUS
That sir is the prudence.

GOTHARUS
Yet I can direct thee
To be reveng'd with safety unto this,
What if I add therein, thou shalt do service
That will oblige the common-wealth, that groans
With fear of innovation, and make
The King thy friend by one expence of courage;
And having nam'd the king thus, it must make
Thy thoughts secure from future losse, and in
The present act no danger.

ALBINA
Sir, be cleere,
Make good what you have promis'd,
And see if I be frighted, I have help'd
Many give up the ghost.

GOTHARUS
Olaus us'd
Thee basely, how much would the Kingdome suffer
If he were dead and laid into his Tombe,
Perhaps a year sooner then nature meant,
To make his bones fit.

AQUINUS
I dare kill him sir,
If I were sure the King would pardon me,
That in my own revenge, and any other
Whom he calls enemy without exception,
To this I am bound in conscience; sir, there needs
No conjuration for this, nor art
To heighten me, let me but hear the King
Will have it, and secure me.

GOTHARUS
Thou deserv'st him,
And maist a statue, for our great deliverer,

Yet, now I have thought better on't, we may
Save trouble in Olaus Tragedy,
And kill him through another.

AQUINUS
Whom?

GOTHARUS
One that
Sits heavier on the Kings heart, and dwels in't
Such a disease, as if no resolute hand
Cure him.

AQUINUS
I'le be his Chyrurgion.

GOTHARUS
When I name him,
One that has had no will to advance thee
To thy deserts in wars, for all thy former
And thy late services, rewarded with
A dull command of Captain, but incenst
By Olaus now who rules his heart, lesse hope
To be repair'd in fortune.

ALBINA
Let him be the Prince.

GOTHARUS
'Tis he.

ALBINA
It honours my attempt;
And while his father holds him disobedient,
I think him lesse then subject.

GOTHARUS
Disobedient? look there.

[Shews a Letter.

AQUINUS
This is the Princes hand.

GOTHARUS
But read his heart.

[**AQUINUS** reads.

AQUINUS

Impious! above the reach
Of common faith.
I am satisfied, he must not live; the way:
They would not trust me with his cup to poyson it,
Shew me the way— the King and Queen.

GOTHARUS

Lets study.

[Enter **KING** and **QUEEN**.

QUEEN MARPISA

You have a faithful servant in Gotharus.

KING

Upon his wisdome we depend.

GOTHARUS

I have it,
He shall dye like a Souldier, thus—[Whispers].

QUEEN MARPISA

Their malice
Doth onely aime at me, and if you please
To give me up a sacrifice to their fury.

KING

Not for a thousand Sons, my life and honors
Must sit with thine Marpisa.

AQUINUS

Sir, 'tis done.

GOTHARUS

This act shall make thee great, the King and Queen
Look cheerefull royal sir, and think of honour
To crown the merit of this Captain, let
No trouble shake a thought, he will deserve
Your bosome sir.

KING

He shall possesse it; how my Gotharus?

GOTHARUS

Pray leave it to me, it is not ripe yet for your knowledge sir.

KING
We'l trust thee, come Marpisa.

GOTHARUS
Dearest Madam! come Aquinus.

AQUINUS
I attend your Lorship.

[Exeunt.

An Apartment in the Palace.

[Enter **HARALDUS, SUENO, HELGA,** at a banquet set out.

SUENO
My Lord, you honour us.

HELGA
If we knew how to expresse our duties.

HARALDUS
No more ceremony,
Your loves engage me, if some discontents
Make me not seem unpleasant; yet I must
Confesse I was more prompted to th'acceptance,
In hope to cure a melancholly.

HORMENUS
With your pardon,
It does too much usurpe on your sweet nature,
But if your Lordship please, there is a way
To banish all those thoughts.

HARALDUS
I would call him doctor
That could assure me that.

SUENO
I am of his
Opinion sir, and know the best receipt
I'th world for sadness.

HARALDUS

Prethee what?

SUENO
Good wine.

HARALDUS
I have heard 'em talk so, If I thought there were
That operation—

HELGA
Try sir.

SUENO
My humble duty—

[Drinks.

'Tis excellent wine!

HARALDUS
Helga.

HELGA
Your Lordships servant.

HARALDUS
'Tis pleasant.

[Drinks.

SUENO
It has spirit, will you please
Another tryall, that prepares more sweetness,
Health to the Queen!

[Drinks.

HARALDUS
I thank you.

HELGA
With your pardon, fill to me,
Your grace should have it last.

HARALDUS
She is my mother.

SUENO

She is our royall mistress, heaven preserve her;
Does not your Lordship feel more inclination

[**HARALDUS** drinks.

To mirth, there is no spell 'gainst sorrow, like
Two or three cups of wine.

HELGA
Nothing believ't,
Will make your soul so active, take it liberally.

HARALDUS
I dare not trust my brain.

SUENO
You never tryed.

HELGA
You'l never know the pleasure then of drinking
I have drunk my selfe into an Emperour.

SUENO
In thy own thoughts.

HELGA
Why is't not rare, that wine
Taken to the extent, should so delightfully
Possess the imagination, I have had my Queens
And Concubines—

HARALDUS
Fine fancies.

HELGA
The Kings health,
Give me't in greater volum, these are acorns
Sueno to thee, I'me sprightly but to look out.

[Drinks.

SUENO
What rare things will the flowing vertue raise,
If but, the sight exalt you? to your grace,
The Kings health.

HARALDUS
Let it come, i'le trespasse once.

HELGA
That smile became you sir.

HARALDUS
This Cup doth warm me,

[Drinks.

Methinks I could be merry.

SUENO
Will your grace have any musick?

HARALDUS
Any thing.

HELGA
Strike lustily.

[Musicke within.

HARALDUS
I have begun no health yet Gentlemen.

SUENO
Now you must honour us.

HARALDUS
Health to the Prince.

HELGA
That is your title sir,
As you are Sonne to a Queen,

HARALDUS
My father was no King, father? i'le drown
The memory of that name.

[Drinkes.

HELGA
The Prince Turgesius health.

SUENO
He's not far off
By the Court Computation—happinesse now
To Prince Haraldus mistress.

HELGA
With devotion.

HARALDUS
Alas, I am too young to have a mistress.

HELGA
Sir, you must crown it.

HARALDUS
These are complements
At Court, where none must want a drinking mistress.

SUENO
Methinks loud musick should attend these Healths—

HARALDUS
So! shall we dance?

[Drinks.

HELGA
We want Ladies.

HARALDUS
I am as light;

[Dances.

—Thou shalt go for a Lady.

SUENO
Shall I?

[Dance.

Is not this better, then to sigh away
Our spirits now?

HARALDUS
I'm hot.

HELGA
A cup of wine is the most naturall cooler.

HARALDUS
You are my Physitians, Gentlemen.

[Drinks.

SUENO
Make it a health, sir, to my Lord Gotharus.
I'le pledge it as heartily as he were my father.

HARALDUS
Whose father?

[Throws the wine in **SUENO'S** face.

SUENO
Mine, I said.

HARALDUS
Cry mercy.

SUENO
Nay, 'tis but so much wine lost, fill't again.

HARALDUS
I'le drink no more.

HELGA
What think you of a song?

SUENO
A catch, to't boyes.

[Song.

HARALDUS
Shall we to bed Gentlemen?
I did not sleep last night.

HELGA
If your Grace
Desire to sleep, there's nothing to prepare it
Like to 'ther cup.

HARALDUS
A health to both your Mistresses.

[Drinks.

SUENO
You do us grace.

HELGA
There's hope of his conversion.

HARALDUS
I am not well, what wheels are in my brains?
Philosophy affirms the earth moves not,
'Tis here me thinks confuted, Gentlemen,
You must be faine to lead me to some couch,
Where I may take a nap, and then i'le thank you,
I'le come agen to morrow.

SUENO
Every day
For a twelve-month.

HELGA
That will make you a good fellow.

[Exit.

SCENE IV

The Country.

[Enter **PRINCE TURGESIUS, REGINALDUS, SOULDIERS** marching, **OLAUS** meets, they salute and whisper.

PRINCE
You tell me wonders.

OLAUS
'Tis all truth, we must
Stand on our guard, 'tis well we are provided.

PRINCE
Is it not some device to make us feare,
That at our entertainment we may find
Our joyes more spatious.

OLAUS
There is some device in't.

PRINCE
It is not possible a father should
Be so unkind to his own blood and honour.

OLAUS
My life was threatned.

PRINCE
Who durst threaten it?

OLAUS
The King your father.

PRINCE
Oh say not so good sir.

OLAUS
And if you please him not with your behaviour,
Your head may be soon humbled to the axe,
And sent a token of his love, to your stepdame
The Queen, I trifle not.

PRINCE
For what sinnes
Hath angry heaven decreed to punish Norway,
And lay the Scene of wrath in her own bowels?
I did suspect when none came forth to meet
Our victory, to have heard of some mis-fortune,
Some prodigies egendring: down with all
Our pride of war, the Garlands we bring home
Will but adorne us for the sacrifice;
And while our hairs are deck'd with flowers and ribbands,
We shall but march more gloriously to death.
Are all good women dead within the Kingdom,
There could be found none worth my fathers love,
But one whose fame and honour is suspected?

OLAUS
Woulst they were but suspected.

PRINCE
Marpisa?

OLAUS
Her preferment was no doubt
Gotharus act, for which 'tis whisper'd,
She payes him fair conditions, while they both
Case up the Kings eyes, or confine him to
Look through such cunning opticks as they please.

PRINCE
I'le have his heart.

OLAUS
But how will you come by't?
He's safe in the Kings bosome, who keeps warm
A serpent, till he find a time to gnaw
Out his preserver.

PRINCE
We had dyed with honour
By the Enemies sword, something might have been read
In such a fall, as might have left no shame
Upon our story, since 'tis chance of war,
Not want of valour, gives the victory;
This ship-wracks all, and eates into the soule
Of all our fame, it withers all the deeds
Is owing to our name.

[Enter **CORTES**.

CORTES
Health to the Prince,

OLAUS
Cortes, welcome, what news?

CORTES
These Letters will inform his highness.

OLAUS
Sent, from the King Cortes? has he thought upon't?
Are we considerable at last, and shall
The Lady Geugaw, that is pearch'd upon
His throne, be counsell'd not to take too much
Upon her? will Gotharus give us leave
To be acquainted with the King agen? ha!

CORTES
These Letters came sir from Aquinus.

OLAUS
How?
I hope he mentions not the broken pate
I gave him, and complains on't to the Prince,
I may be apt to make him an amends
With such another.

PRINCE
Sir.

OLAUS
What's the matter?

PRINCE
Read, I am planet-stroke, cursed Gotharus!
What would the traytor have?

OLAUS
'Tis here, I take it, he would have you sent
Yonder, and has tooke order with Aquinus
For your conveyance hence, at both their charges;
But now you know the plot, you wo' not trust
Your life as he directs.

PRINCE
Not trust Aquinus?

OLAUS
You are desperate, hark you, I do suspect him,
And I ha' cause, I broke his head at Court
For his impertinent counsell, when I was
In passion with the King, you sha'not trust him,
This may be cunning to revenge himselfe,
I know he has a spirit, come you sha' not
Be cheated of your life, while I have one
To counsell you.

PRINCE
Uncle, I am unmov'd,
He is a Souldier, to that name and honour
I'le trust a Princes life, he dares not be
A traytor.

OLAUS
I have read that one Prince was
So credulous, and scap'd, but Alexander,
Though he were great, was not so wise a Gentleman,
As heaven in that occasion might have made him,
The valiant confidence in his doctor, might
Ha' gnawn his bowels up, and where had been
My gallant Macedonian? come you shall
Consider on't.

PRINCE
I am resolv'd already,
March to the City, every thought doth more
Confirm me, passion will not let you see,

Good Uncle with your pardon, the true worth
And inside of Aquinus, he is faithfull,
Should I miscarry, 'tis my single life,
And 'tis obedience to give up our breath,
When fathers shall conspire their Childrens death

[Exeunt.

ACT IV

SCENE I

The Palace.

Enter **KING** and **GOTHARUS**.

GOTHARUS
You may surrender up your Crown, 'twell shew
Brave on Turgesius Temples, whose ambition
Expects it.

KING
Nay Gotharus—

GOTHARUS
Has my care
Cast to prevent your shame, how to preserve
The glories you possesse, by cutting off
A Canker that would eat into your trunck,
And hinder your fair growth, and do you make
A scruple to be cured?

KING
I did but mention,
And nature may excuse, he is my son.

GOTHARUS
The more your danger, when he dares be impious,
The forfeit of his duty in this bold
And hostile manner to affright your subjects,
And threaten you with articles, is already
The killing of your honour, and a treason
Nature abhors, a guilt heaven trembles at,
And you are bound in care of your own province,
To shew your justice, and not be partiall
To your own blood; but let your Kingdome suffer,

Her heart be torn by civill Wars; 'tis none
Of mine, and let him in the blood of many
Fathers, be made a King, your King; and you
That now command, be taught obedience,
Creep to your child, exchange your pallace for
A prison, and be humbled till you think
Death a preferment, I have but a life—

KING
Which I will cherish, be not passionate,
And I consent to all thou hast contained;
Thou art my friend.

GOTHARUS
I would be sir, your honest Chyrurgion,
And when you have a Gangrene in your limb,
Not flatter you to death, but tell you plainly
If you would live, the part so poyson'd must be
Cut from your body.

KING
And I wo'not shake
With horror of the wound, but meet my safety
And thank my best preserver; but art sure
Aquinus will be resolute?

GOTHARUS
Suspect not,
He is my Creature.

[Enter **HORMENUS**.

HORMENUS
The Prince your Sonne—

KING
Is a bold Traytor.
And they are Rebels joyne with him.

GOTHARUS
What of the Prince Hormenus?

HORMENUS
He is very near the City with his Army.

KING
Are the walls fortified?

HORMENUS
They are?

KING
We wo'not trust him, nor the Ruffian
Olaus, that Incendiary.

GOTHARUS
The Queen.

[Enter **QUEEN MARPISA**.

QUEEN MARPISA
O sir.

KING
There are more wounds in those sad accents,
Then their rebellion can give my Kingdome.

QUEEN MARPISA
My boy, my child, Haraldus.

KING
What of him?

QUEEN MARPISA
Is sick, is dying sir.

GOTHARUS
Forbid it heavens, he was in health—

QUEEN MARPISA
But if I mean to see him
A live, they say I must make hast,
The comforts of my life expire with him.

[Exit.

GOTHARUS
The Devils up in arms, and fates conspire
Against us.

KING
Mischiefes tumble like waves upon us.

HORMENUS
Sir, It will be necessary
You lend your person to direct, what shall

Be further done i'th City, Aquinus hath
Charge of the Gate and Walls, that offer
The first view to the Enemy.

KING
He is trusty, and
A daring Souldier; what at stand Gotharus?

GOTHARUS
I was thinking of the Queen sir, and Haraldus,
And grieve for the sweet child.

KING
Some feaver, would my
Son were in his state, but soon we shall
Conclude his destiny, if Aquinus prosper;
But to the walls.

GOTHARUS
I attend, my very soule
Is in a sweat, Hormenus.

HORMENUS
I wait on you.

[Exeunt:

SCENE II

Before the Walls of the City.

[Enter **PRINCE TURGESIUS, OLAUS, CORTES, REGINALDUS, SOULDIERS.**

PRINCE
The Gates are shut against us Souldiers.

OLAUS
Let our Engines
Teare 'em, and batter down the walls.

PRINCE
Good Uncle,
Your counsell I obey'd i'th wars abroad,
We did there fight for honour, and might use
All the most horrid formes of death to fright
Our enemies, and cut our way to victory:

But give me leave to tell you sir, at home
Our conquest will be losse, and every wound
We give our Country, is a crimson teare
From our own heart, they are a viperous brood
Gnaw through the bowels of their parent, I
Will rather dye without a monument,
Then have it bear my name, to have defaced
One heap of stones.

[Enter **GOTHARUS** on the walls with **HORMENUS AQUINUS**.

CORTES
Gotharus on the walls?

OLAUS
Hormonus and Aquinus? now a speech,
And 'twere at Gallowes would become him better.

GOTHARUS
Thus from my master, to the Prince of Norway,
We did expect, and had prepar'd to meet
Your victory with triumphs, and with Garlands
Due to your fate and valours, entertain'd you.
Nor has your Army sacrific'd so many
Warm drops of blood, as we have shot up prayers
That you might prosper, and return the pledge
Of all our hope and glory. But when pride
Of your own fames, and conquest in a war,
Hath poyson'd the obedience of a Sonne,
And tempted you to advance your sword, new bath'd
In enemies blood 'gainst your Countries bosome;
Thus we receive you, and declare your pietie,
And faith lost to your Country, and your Father.

PRINCE
My Lord, all this concerns not me, we have
But done our dutyes, and return to lay
The Trophies at his feet, whose justice did
Make us victorious more then our own valour,
And now without all titles but his sonne,
I dare hells accusation, to blast
My humble thoughts.

GOTHARUS
Sir, give us leave to feare,
Not your own nature, calme as the soft aire,
When no rude wind conspires a mutiny—

OLAUS

Leave Rethorique, and to'th point, why do not
The Gates spread to receive us? and your joyes
Shoot up in acclamations? I would have
Thy house give good example to the City
And make us the first-born fire.

GOTHARUS

Good heaven knows,
How willingly I would sacrifice my selfe,
To do a gratefull service to the Prince:
And I could wish my Lord, you were less passionate,
And not inflame his Highnesse gentle spirit
To these attempts.

PRINCE

I am ignorant Gotharus
Of what you mean, where is the King my father?

AQUINUS

Where a sad father is, to know his Sonne
Bring arms against his life.

PRINCE

How now Aquinus,

OLAUS

Dare you be saucy?
O that Gentleman
Is angry, his head akes with the remembrance of
My Truncheon.

AQUINUS

'Twas a valiant act,
And did become the greatness of Olaus,
Who by the priviledge of his birth, may do
A wrong and boast it.

OLAUS

Shall these Groomes affront us?

PRINCE

Have you commission to be thus insolent,
They do not know us?

GOTHARUS

Yes, and in our hearts
Bleed, that our fears of your unjust demand,

Compell us to this separation.

PRINCE
Demands? is it injustice for a Sonne
To aske his fathers blessing? by thy duty
Gotharus, I command thee, tell my father
His Sonne desires access, let me but speak with him.

GOTHARUS
I have not in your absence sir neglected,
What did become my service to your highnesse,
To take his anger off.

PRINCE
What Riddles this?

GOTHARUS
But let me with a pardon tell your Grace,
The Letters that you sent, were not so dutyfull,
You were to blame, to chide and Article
So with a King and Father; yet I said,
And pawn'd my Conscience 'twas no act of yours,
I mean intyre, but wrought and form'd by some
Rash spirits, to corrupt you with ambition,
Feeding your youth with thought of hasty empire
To serve their ends, whose counsell all this while
Did starve that sweetness in you we all hop'd for.

OLAUS
Devices! more devices!

PRINCE
I am amaz'd,
And if the King will not vouchsafe me conference,
I shall accuse thy cunning to have poyson'd
My Fathers good opinion.

[Enter **KING** on the walls.

GOTHARUS
Innocence
May thus be stain'd, pray let your justice clear me.

KING
What would our Sonne?

PRINCE
Thus pay his filiall duty.

[Kneels.

KING
'Tis but counterfet, if you bring no thought
To force our blessing in this rude manner, how
Dare you approach? dismiss your souldiers.

OLAUS
Not the meanest knapsack,
That were a way to bring us to the mercy
Of wolves indeed, Gotharus grinds his teeth
Already at us.

KING
We shall talk with you sir
Hereafter, I command thee by thy duty
Thou ow'st a father and a King, dismiss
Your Troops.

PRINCE
I will.

OLAUS
You shall not, that were fine,
So we may run our heads into their noose,
You give away your safty.

PRINCE
I will not
Dispute my power, let my intreat prevaile
For their dimission.

OLAUS
You may dimiss
Your head and mine, and be laugh'd at, these men
Are honest, and dare fight for us.

PRINCE
I know
Their loves, and will rewait; dear, dear Uncle.

GOTHARUS
How he prepares his Tragedy Aquinus,
Let not thy hand shake.

AQUINUS
I am resolute.

GOTHARUS
And i, for thy reward.

[Exeunt **SOULDIERS**.

'Tis done, the souldiers
Disperse already.

OLAUS
If any mischiefe follow this,
Thank your credulitie.

PRINCE
May I now hope for access?

KING
Descend Gotharus and Aquinus
To meet the Prince, while he containes within
The piety of a Son, we shall imbrace him.

PRINCE
When I degenerate, let me be accurst
By heaven and you.

OLAUS
Are you not pale to think on't.

PRINCE
It puzzels me to think my father guilty.

OLAUS
I do not like things yet.

[As the **PRINCE** is going forth, a Pistoll is discharged within, he falls.

PRINCE
O I am shot, I am murder'd.

OLAUS
Inhumane Trayton, villaine.

[**OLAUS** wounds **AQUINUS**.

GOTHARUS
So, so, his hand has saved my execution,
'Tis not safe for me to stay, they are both sped rarely.

[Exit.

OLAUS
O my dear Cousin, treason, treason.

KING
Where?

OLAUS
In thy own bosome, thou hast kil'd thy Sonne,
Convey his body, guard it safe, and this
Perfidious trunke i'le have it punish't
Past death, and scatter his torn flesh about
The world to affright mankind. [To the **KING**] Thou art
A murthdren, no blood of mine

GOTHARUS
'Tis done,
And all the guilt dyes with Aquinus, falne
By Olaus sword most happily, who but
Prevented mine, this act concludes all feare.

KING
He was my sonne, I must needs drop a teare.

[Exeunt.

SCENE III

An Apartment in the Palace.

[**HARALDUS** discovered sick, **QUEEN MARPISA, DOCTORS.**

QUEEN MARPISA
It is not possible, he has such a feavor
By excess of wine? he was all temperance.

DOCTOR
He had a soft and tender constitution,
Apt to be inflam'd, they that are most abstemious,
Feel the disorder with more violence.

QUEEN MARPISA
Where, who assisted him in this mis-fortune?
He had some company.

DOCTOR

He was invited
He sayes by Sueno, and Helga, to a banquet,
Where in their mirth, they careless of his health,
Suffered him drink too much.

QUEEN MARPISA

They poyson'd him,
Go apprehend the murtherers of my child,
If he recover not, their death shall wait
Upon Haraldus; but pray you tell me Gentlemen,
Is there no hope of life, have you not art
Enough to cure a feavor?

DOCTOR

We find Madam,
His disease more malignant by some thought
Or apprehensions of griefe.

QUEEN MARPISA

What griefe?
Y'are all impostors, and are Ignorant
But how to kill.

HARALDUS

Is not my mother come?

QUEEN MARPISA

Yes my deare sonne, and here shall weep my selfe
Till I turne Niobe, unlesse thou givest me
Some hope of thy own life.

HARALDUS

I would say something
Were you alone.

QUEEN MARPISA

Leave us;—

[Exeunt **PHYSICIANS**.

Now my Haraldus,
How is it with my child?

HARALDUS

I know you love me,
Yet I must tell you truth, I cannot live,
And let this comfort you, death will not come

Unwelcome to your sonne, I do not dye
Against my will, and having my desires,
You have less cause to mourne.

QUEEN MARPISA
What is't has made
The thought of life unpleasant, which does court
Thy dwelling here with all delights that nature
And art can study for thee, rich in all things
Thy wish can be ambitious of, yet all
These treasures nothing to thy mothers love,
Which to enjoy thee would defer a while
Her thought of going to heaven.

HARALDUS
Oh take heed mother, heaven
Has a spatious eare and power to punish,
Your too much love with my eternal absence,
I begge your prayers and blessing.

QUEEN MARPISA
Th'art dejected,
Have but a will and live.

HARALDUS
'Tis in vaine mother.

QUEEN MARPISA
Sinke with a feavour into earth?
Look up, thou shalt not dye.

HARALDUS
I have a wound within
You do not see, more killing then all feavors.

QUEEN MARPISA
A wound? where? who has murder'd thee?

HARALDUS
Gotharus—

QUEEN MARPISA
Ha! furies persecute him.

HARALDUS
Oh pray for him!
'Tis my duty, though he gave me death,
He is my father.

QUEEN MARPISA
How? thy father?

HARALDUS
He told me so, and with that breath destroy'd me,
I felt it strike upon my spirits; mother,
Would I had neer been born!

QUEEN MARPISA
Believe him not.

HARALDUS
Oh do not add another sinne to what
Is done already, death is charitable
To quit me from the scorn of all the world.

QUEEN MARPISA
By all my hopes Gotharus has abus'd thee,
Thou art the lawful burden of my wombe,
Thy father, Altomarus.

HARALDUS
Ha!

QUEEN MARPISA
Before whose spirit long since taken up,
To meet with Saints and Troops Angelicall,
I dare agen repeat thou art his Sonne.

HARALDUS
Ten thousand blessings now reward my mother!
Speake it againe, and I may live, a stream
Of pious joy runnes through me, to my soule
Y'ave stroke a harmony next that in heaven;
Can you without a blush, call me your Child,
And sonne of Altomarus? all that's holy
Dwell in your blood for ever, speak it once,
But once agen.

QUEEN MARPISA
Were it my latest breath,
Thou art his and mine.
Enough, my tears do flow
To give you thanks for't; I would you could resolve me
But one truth more, why did my Lord Gotharus
Call me the issue of his blood?

QUEEN MARPISA
Alas, he thinks thou art—

HARALDUS
What are those words? I am undone
Agen.

QUEEN MARPISA
Ha!

HARALDUS
'Tis too late to call 'em back, he thinks I am his son—

QUEEN MARPISA
I have confess'd too much, and tremble with
The imagination, forgive me child,
And heaven, if there be mercy to a crime
So black, as I must now to quit thy fears,
Say I have been guilty off, we have been sinful,
And I was not unwilling to oblige
His active braine for thy advancement, by
Abusing his beliefe thou wer't his own,
But thou hast no such staine, thy birth is innocent,
Or may I perish ever, 'tis a strange
Confession to a child, but it may drop
A balsome to thy wound; live my Haraldus,
If not for this, to see my penitence,
And with what tears i'le wash away my sinne.

HARALDUS
I am no bastard then.

QUEEN MARPISA
Thou art not.

HARALDUS
But I am not found while you are lost,
No time can restore you,
My spirits faint.

QUEEN MARPISA
Will nothing comfort thee?

HARALDUS
My duty to the Kign.

QUEEN MARPISA
He's here.

[Enter **KING**.

KING
How is't Haraldus?
Death sits in's face.

HARALDUS
Give me you blessing, and within my heart
Ile pray you may have many, my soul flyes
'Bove this vain world, good Mother close mine eyes.

[He dies.

QUEEN MARPISA
Never dyed so much sweetnesse in his years.

KING
Be comforted, I have lost my sonne too,
The Prince is slaine, how now.

[Enter **OFFICERS** with **HELGA**.

QUEEN MARPISA
Justice upon the murderer of my sonne,
This villaine Helga, and his companion
Sueno, have kil'd him, where's the other?

OFFICER
Fled Madam,
But Helga does confesse he made him drunk.

HELGA
But not dead drunk, I do beseech you Madam.

KING
Look here what your base surfet has destroy'd.

HELGA
'Twas Sueno as well as I, my Lord Gotharus
Gave us commission for what we did.

QUEEN MARPISA
Again Gotharus, sure he plotted this.

KING
Hang him up straight.

HELGA

I left no drink behind me,
If I must dye let me have equall justice,
And let one of your guard drink me to death sir;
Or if you please to let me live till
Sueno is taken, we will drink and reele
Out of the world together.

KING

Hence, and hang him.

[Exeunt **OFFICERS** with **HELGA**.

[Enter **HORMENUS**.

HORMENUS

Sir, you must make provision against
New danger, discontent is broke into
A wild rebellion, and many of your subjects
Gather in tumults, and give out they will
Revenge the Princes death.

KING

This I did feare,
Where's Gotharus? O my fright, my conscience,
Has furies in't, where's Gotharus?—

HORMENUS

Not in the Court.

KING

I tremble with confusions.

[Exit **KING** and **HORMENUS**.

QUEEN MARPISA

I am resolv'd, my joyes are all expir'd,
Nor can ambition more concern me now,
Gotharus has undone me in the death
Of my loved Sonne, his fate is next, while I
Move resolute i'le command his destiny.

[Exit.

SCENE IV

A Room in Gotharus's House.

[Enter **GOTHARUS**.

HORMENUS
How are we lost, the Prince Turgesius death
Is of no use, since 'tis unprofitable
To the great hope we stored up in Haraldus,
It was a cursed plot directed me
To raise his spirit, by those giddy engines
That have undone him, their souls reel to hell for't
How will Marpisa weep her selfe into
The obscure shades, and leave me here to grow
A statue with the wonder of our fate.

[Enter **ALBINA**.

ALBINA
Sir.

GOTHARUS
Do not trouble me.

ALBINA
Although
I am not partner of your joyes or comfort,
Yet let your cruelty be so mindfull of me
I may divide your sorrows.

GOTHARUS
Would thy sufferings
Could ease me of the weight, I would
Empty my heart of all that's ill, to sinke thee,
And bury thee alive, thy sight is hatefull,
Aske me not why, but in obedience
Fly hence into some wildernesse. The Queeen.

[Enter **QUEEN MARPISA**.

[Exit **ALBINA**.

GOTHARUS
Great Queen, did any sorrow lade my bosome,
But what does almost melt it for Haraldus,
Your presence would revive me, but it seems
Our hopes and joyes in him grew up so mighty,
Heaven became jealous, we should undervalue
The bliss of th'other world, and build in him

A richer Paradice.

QUEEN MARPISA
I have mourn'd already
A mothers part, and fearing thy excess
Of griefe, present my selfe to comfort thee,
Tears will not call him back, and 'twill become us
Since we two are the world unto our selves,
(Nothing without the circle of our arm's
Precious and welcome) to take heed our griefe
Make us not oversoon, like him that dead,
And our blood useless.

GOTHARUS
Were you present Madam,
When your Sonne dyed?

QUEEN MARPISA
I was.

GOTHARUS
And did you weepe;
And wish him live, and would not heaven at
Your wish, return his wandering Ghost agen?
Your voyce should make another out of Atomes;
I do adore the harmony, and from
One pleasant look, draw in more blessings
Then death knows how to kill.

MARPISA [aside]
He is recovered from his passion.

GOTHARUS
Whats this? Ha!

QUEEN MARPISA
Where?

GOTHARUS
Here, like a sudden winter
Struck on my heart, I am not well o'th sudden, Ha!

QUEEN MARPISA
My Lord, make use of this, 'tis Cordial,

[Gives him a box of poyson.

I am often subject to these passions,

And dare not walk without this Ivory box
To prevent danger, they are pleasant,
'Tis a most happy opportunity.

GOTHARUS
Let me present my thanks to my preserver,

[Enter **ALBINA**.

And kiss your hand.

QUEEN MARPISA
Our lips will meet more lovingly.

ALBINA
My heart will break.

QUEEN MARPISA
Your Lady, we are betray'd,
She see us kiss, and I shall hate her for't.

GOTHARUS
Does this offend your vertue?

ALBINA
Y'are merciless,
You shall be a less Tyrant sir to kill me,
Injurious Queen!

QUEEN MARPISA
Shall I be here affronted?
I shall not think Gotharus worth my love,
To let her breath forth my dishonour, which
Her passion hath already dared to publish,
Nor wanted she before an impudence
To throw this poyson in my face.

GOTHARUS
I'le tame her.

[Exit.

ALBINA
I wo'not curse you Madam, but you are
The Cruel'st of all woman kind,
I am prepared to meet your tyrannies.

[Enter **GOTHARUS** with a Pistol, at the other door, a **SERVANT**.

SERVANT
My Lord,
We are undone, the common people are
In arms, and violently assault our house,
Threatning your Lordship with a thousand deaths,
For the good Prince, whose murther they exclaime
Contriv'd by you.

GOTHARUS
The frends of hell will shew more mercy to me,
Where shall I hide me?

QUEEN MARPISA
Alas they'l kill me too.

[Exit.

SERVANT
There's no staying, they have broke the wall of the first Court,
Down at some window sir.

[**GOTHARUS** drops the pistol which **ALBINA** takes up.

GOTHARUS
Helpe me, O help me, I am lost.

[Exit with **SERVANT**.

[Within—
Down with the doors,
This way, this way.

[Enter **REBELS**.

ALBINA [Presents the Pistol]
He that first moves this way
Comes on his death, I can dispatch but one,
And take your choise.

1ST REBEL
Alas good Madam, we do not come to trouble you
You have sorrow enough, we would talk
With my Lord your pagan husband.

2ND REBEL
I, I, where is he?

3ʳᴰ REBEL
That Traytor.

4ᵀᴴ REBEL
Murderer of our Prince.

ALBINA
Y'are not well informed,
Aquinus kill'd the Prince.

2ᴺᴰ REBEL
But by my Lords correction
We know his heart, and do meane to eat it.
Therefore let him appeare, knock down the Lady
You with the long bill.

ALBINA
How dare you runne the hazard of your lives
And fortunes, thus like out-laws, without authority
To break into our houses, when you have done,
What fury leads you to 't, you will buy too dear
Repentance at the Gallows.

2ᴺᴰ REBEL
Hang the Gallowes, and give us my Lord your husband.

[Enter **SERVANT**.

SERVANT
He's escap'd Madam, now they may search.

[Enter more **REBELS**.

ALBINA
But where's the Queen, she must not be betrai'd.

1ˢᵀ REBEL
This way, this way, he got out of a window,
And leap'd a wall, follow, follow!

[Exeunt **REBELS**.

[**Within**—
Follow, follow, follow.

ALBINA
O my poor Gotharus.

[Enter **QUEEN MARPISA**.

ALBINA
Madam, you are secure, though you pursued
My death, I wish you safety,

QUEEN MARPISA
I have been
Too cruell, but my fate compell'd me to't.

[Exit.

ALBINA
I am become the extreamest of all miseries.
Oh my unhappy Lord.

[Exit.

SCENE V

A Street.

[Enter **SUENO**, disguised.

SUENO
Helga is hanged, what will become of me?
I think I were best turn Rebel, there's no hope
To walk without a guard, and that I shall not
Want to the Gallowes, heathen Halberdiers
Are used to have a care, and do rejoyce
To see men have good ends.

[Enter **GOTHARUS**.

GOTHARUS
I am pursued.

SUENO
My Lord Gotharus? worse and worse, oh for a mist before his eyes.

GOTHARUS
You sha'not betray me sir.

[Draws a poniard.

SUENO

Hold my Lord, I am your servant, honest Sueno.

GOTHARUS
Sueno, off with that case, it may secure me,
Quickly, or—

SUENO
Oh my Lord, you shall command my skin,
Alas poor Gentleman, I'm glad I have it
To do your Lordship service.

GOTHARUS
Nay, your beard too?

SUENO
Yes, yes, any thing:
Alas my good Lord, how comes this?

GOTHARUS
Leave your untimely prating, help!

[They exchange dresses.

You'll not betray me?

SUENO
I'le first be hanged.

[Within]
—Follow, follow.

GOTHARUS
Hell stop their throats; so, so, now thy reward

SUENO
It was my duty, troth sir I will have nothing.

GOTHARUS
Yes, take that, and that, for killing of Haraldus.

[Wounds him.

Now I'm sure you will not prate.

SUENO
O murder!

[Within

—Follow, follow.

GOTHARUS
I cannot escape. Oh help invention!

[He bloodies himself with **SUENO'S** blood, and falls down as dead.

[Enter **REBELS**.

1ˢᵗ REBEL
This way they say he went, what's he?

2ᴺᴰ REBEL
One of our company I think,

3ᴿᴰ REBEL
Who kil'd him?

4ᵀᴴ REBEL
I know not.

2ᴺᴰ REBEL
Lets away, if we can find that Traytor,
He shall pay for all.

4ᵀᴴ REBEL
Oh that I had him here, I'de teach him—

2ᴺᴰ REBEL
This way, this way.

SUENO
Oh.

[**GOTHARUS** rises and steals away.

3ᴿᴰ REBEL
Stay, There's one groans.

SUENO
Oh—

2ᴺᴰ REBEL
Nay 'twas here abouts, another dead?

4ᵀᴴ REBEL
He has good cloathes, Gotharus? the very cur.

3RD REBEL
'Tis Gotharus, I have seen the dog.

2ND REBEL
'Tis he, 'tis he.

SUENO
Oh.

[Exit **GOTHARUS**.

2ND REBEL
Now 'tis not he, if thou canst speak my friend—

SUENO
Gotharus murdered me, and shifted cloathes,
He cannot be far off, oh.

1ST REBEL
Thats he that lyes dead yonder, O that he were
Alive againe, that we might kill him one after another.

3RD REBEL
He's gone:

2ND REBEL
The Devill he is, follow, follow.

3RD REBEL
This way, he cannot scape us, farewell friend,
i'le doe thee a courtecy.
Follow, follow.

[Exit **REBELS**.

SCENE VI

An Apartment in Olaus' House, with a Coffin in it.

[Enter **OLAUS, PRINCE, AQUINUS** and **CORTES**.

OLAUS
So, so, in this disguise you may to'th Army,
Who though they seem to scatter, are to meet
By my directions, honest Aquinus, you
You wait on the Prince, but sir—[Whispers].

CORTES
Were you not wounded?

AQUINUS
I prepared a privie Coat, for that I knew Gotharus
Would have been too busie with my flesh else,
But he thinks I'm slaine by the Duke, and hugges
His fortune in't.

PRINCE
You'l follow.

OLAUS
And bring you news, perhaps the Rabble are
In hot pursuite after the Polititian,
He cannot scape them, they'l teare him like
So many hungry Mastives.

[Exit.

PRINCE
I could wish they had him.

OLAUS
Lose no time, Cortes stay you with me,
Not that I think my house will want your guard.

CORTES
Command me sir.

OLAUS
Whas ever such a practise by a father,
To take away his Sonnes life?

PRINCE
I would hope he may not be so guilty, yet I know not
How his false terrors multiplied by the Art
Of this Gotharus may prevaile upon him,
And win consent.

OLAUS
Aquinus has been faithfull,
And deceived all their treasons, but the Prince
Is still thought dead, this empty Coffine shall
Confirme the people in his funerall,
To keep their thoughts revengeful,

[Within.
Follow, follow—
Till we are possest of him that plotted all.

CORTES
The cry draws this way,
They are excellent Blood-hounds.

[Enter **GOTHARUS**.

GOTHARUS
As you are men, defend me from the rage
Of the devouring multitude; I have
Deserv'd your anger, and a death, but let not
My limbs inhumanely be torne by them,
O save me.

[Within.
Follow, foll—

OLAUS
Blest occasion.

GOTHARUS
I am forced to take your house, and now implore
Your mercy, but to rescue me from them,
And be your own revenger, yet my life
Is worth your preservation for a time,
Do it, and i'le reward you with a story
You'l not repent to know.

OLAUS
You cannot be safe here,
Their rage is high, and every doore
Must be left open to their violence,
Unlesse you will obscure you in this Coffin,
Prepared for the sweet Prince that's murder'd,
And but expects his body which is now imbalming.

GOTHARUS
That, O y'are charitable.

[Within.
Follow, fol—

GOTHARUS
Their noise is Thunder to my soul,

[He goes into the Coffin.

So, so!

[Enter **REBELS.**

OLAUS
How now Gentlemen! what means this Tumult?
Do you know that I possesse this dwelling?

REBEL
Yes my Lord,
But we were told my Lord Gotharus entred,
And we beseech you give him to our justice,
He is the common enemy, and we know he killed the Prince.

OLAUS
You may search if you please,
He can presume of small protection here,
But I much thank you for your loyalties,
And service to the Prince, whose bloodless ruines
Are there, and do but wait when it will please
His father to reverse a cruell sentence,
That keeps him from a buriall with his Ancestors,
We are forbid to do him rights of funerall.

1ST REBEL
How, not bury him?

2ND REBEL
Forbid to bury our good Prince? we'l bury him,
And see what Priest dare not assist us.

3RD REBEL
Not bury him? we'l do't, and carry his body in triumph
Through the City, and see him laid i'th great Tombs

1ST REBEL
Not bury our Prince? that were a jest indeed.

CORTES
'Tis their love and duty.

2ND REBEL
We'l pull the Church down, but we'l have our will.

3RD REBEL
Deare Prince, how sweet he smels.

1ˢᵀ REBEL
Come Countrymen march, and see who dares
Take his body from us.

CORTES
You cannot helpe.

OLAUS
They'l bury him alive.

CORTES
He's in a fright.

OLAUS
So may all Traytors thrive.

[Exeunt **REBELS** with the Coffin followed by **CORTES** and **OLAUS**.

ACT V

SCENE I

An Apartment in the Palace.

Enter **KING** and **QUEEN MARPISA**.

KING
Oh I am lost, and my soul bleeds to thinke
By my own dotage upon thee.

QUEEN MARPISA
I was curst
When I first saw thee, poor wind-shaken King!
I have lost my Sonne.

KING
Thy honour impious woman,
Of more price then a Sonne, or thy own life,
I had a sonne too, whom my rashness sent
To another world, my poor Turgesius,
What sorcery of thy tongue and eyes betraid me?

QUEEN MARPISA
I would I had been a Basilisk, to have shot
A death to thy dissembling heart, when I

Gave my selfe up thy Queen; I was secure,
Till thou with the temptation of greatnesse
And flattery, didst poyson my sweet peace,
And shall thy base feares leave me now a prey
To Rebels?

KING
I had been happy to have left
Thee sooner, but be gone, get to some wildernesse
Peopled with Serpents, and engender with
Some Dragon like thy self.

QUEEN MARPISA
Ha, ha.

KING
Dost laugh thou prodigie? thou shame of woman?

QUEEN MARPISA
Yes, and despise thee dotard, vex till thy soul
Break from thy rotten flesh, I will be merry
At thy last groan.

KING
O my poor boy! my sonne!
His wound is printed here, that false Gotharus,
Your wanton Goat I feare, practis'd with thee
His death.

QUEEN MARPISA
'Twas thy own act and timerous heart, in hope
To be secure, I glory in the mention
Thou murderer of thy sonne.

[Enter **HORMENUS**.

HORMENUS
Oh sir, if ever, stand upon your guard,
The Army which you thought scattered and broke,
Is grown into a great and threatning body,
Lead by the Duke Olaus your lov'd Uncle,
Is marching hither, all your subjects fly to him.

[Exit.

QUEEN MARPISA
Ha! Ha!

KING
Curse on thy spleene, is this a time for laughter,
When horror should afflict thy guilty soule?
Hence mischiefe.

QUEEN MARPISA
Not to obey thee, (shadow of a King)
Am I content to leave thee, and but I wo'not
Prevent thy greater sorrow and vexation,
Now I would kill thee coward.

KING
Treason, treason.

QUEEN MARPISA
I, I, Who comes to your rescue?

KING
Are all fled?

QUEEN MARPISA
Slaves do it naturally.

KING
Canst thou hope to scape?

QUEEN MARPISA
I am mistress of my fate, and do not feare
Their inundation, their Army comming,
It does prepare my triumph, they shall give
Me libertie, and punish thee to live.

KING
Undone, forsaken, miserable King!

[Exeunt severally.

SCENE II

Before the Palace.

[Enter **PRINCE, OLAUS, CORTES, AQUINUS, SOLDIERS.**

PRINCE
Worthy Aquinus, I must honour thee,
Thou hast preserv'd us all, thy service will

Deserve a greater monument then thanks.

AQUINUS
Thank the Duke, for breaking o' my pate.

OLAUS
I know 'twas well bestow'd, but we have now
Proof of thy honest heart.

AQUINUS
But what with your highness favour, do you meane
To do with your father?

PRINCE
Pay my duty to him,
He may be sensible of his cruelty,
And not repent to see me live.

OLAUS
But with your favour, something else must be
Considered, there's a thing he calls his Queen,
A limbe of Lucifer, she must be rosted
For the Armies satisfaction.

AQUINUS
They'l ne'r digest her,
The Kings hounds may be kept hungry
Enough perhaps, and make a feast upon her.

PRINCE
I wonder how the rabble will bestow
The Coffin.

OLAUS
Why, they'l bury him alive
I hope.

PRINCE
Did they suppose my body there?

OLAUS
I'm sorry, he will fare so much the better,
I would the Queen were there to comfort him,
Oh they would smell, and sweat together rarely.

AQUINUS
He dare as soon be damn'd as make a noise,
Or stirre, or cough.

OLAUS
If he should sneeze.

CORTES
'Tis his best course to go into the ground
With silence.

[Trumpet sounded within.

PRINCE
March on, stay, what Trumpets that?

[Enter **REBELS** with a trumpet before the Coffin marching.

OLAUS
They are no enemies, I know the Coffin.

AQUINUS
What rusty Regiment ha' we here?

OLAUS
They are going to bury him, he's not yet discovered;
Oh do not hinder 'em, 'tis a work of charity:
Yet now I do consider better on't,
You may do well to shew your selfe, that may
Be a meanes to waken the good Gentleman,
And make some sport before the rascall smell,
And yet he's in my nostrill, he has perfum'd
His box already.

[The **PRINCE** discovers himself.

OMNES REBELS
'Tis he, 'tis he, the Prince alive! Hey?

[They see the **PRINCE** throw down the Coffin, and run to kneel and embrace him.

AQUINUS
What would he give but for a knife to cut
His own throat now?

OMNES REBELS
Our noble Prince alive?

PRINCE
That owes himselfe to all your loves.

AQUINUS

What? what trinkets ha' you there?

1ST REBEL

The Duke Olaus told us 'twas the Princes body,
Which we resolv'd to bury with magnificence.

AQUINUS

So it appeares.

OLAUS

'Tis better as it is.

2ND REBEL

There's something in't, my shoulder is still sensible,
Lets search, stand off—

OLAUS

Now do you sent him Gentlemen? he wo'd forgive
The hangman to dispatch him out o'th way;
Now will these Masties use him like a Cat,
Most dreadful Rogues at an execution:
Now! now!

[They open the coffin.

1ST REBEL

'Tis a man, ha Gotharus, the thing we whet our teeth for.

OMNES REBELS

Out with the traytor, and with the murderer, hey, drag him.

OLAUS

I told you.

1ST REBEL

Hold, know your dutie fellow renagades,
We do beseech thee high and mighty Prince,
Let us dispose of what we brought, this traytor
He was given us by the Duke, fortune has
Thrown him into our teeth.

OLAUS

And they'l devour him.

OMNES REBELS

We beseech your highness.

OLAUS
I doe acknowledge it, good sir grant their boone,
And try the Caniballs.

2ND REBEL
Ile have an arme.

3RD REBEL
Ile have a legge, I am a Shoomaker,
His shinbone may be useful.

4TH REBEL
I want a signe, give me his head.

PRINCE
Stay, let's first see him, is he not stifled?

3RD REBEL
I had rather my wife were speechlesse.

OLAUS
The Coffin sir was never close.

PRINCE
He does not stirre.

1ST REBEL
We'l make him stir, hang him, he's but asleepe.

2ND REBEL
He's dead, hum.

OLAUS
Dead? Then the Devill is not so wise as I took him.

PRINCE
He's dead, and has prevented all their fury.

AQUINUS
He was not smother'd, the Coffin had aire enough.

OLAUS
He might ha' liv'd to give these Gentlemen some content.

1ST REBEL
Oh let us teare his limbs.

PRINCE

Let none use any violence to his body,
I feare he has met reward above your punishment.

2ND REBEL
Let me have but his clothes.

3RD REBEL
He is a Taylor.

2ND REBEL
Onely to cut out a sute for a Tarytor by 'em,
Or any man, my conscience would wish hang'd.

4TH REBEL
Let me have a button for a relique—

PRINCE
No more.

OLAUS
There is some mystery in his death.

[Enter **KING**.

The King? obscure a little nephew—

[The **PRINCE** retires.

KING
To whom now must I kneel? where is the King?
For I am nothing, and deserve to be so,
Unto you Uncle must I bow, and give
My Crown, pray take it, with it give me leave
To tell you, what it brings the hapless wearer,
Beside the outside glory: for I am
Read in the miserable fate of Kings.
You thinke it glorious to command, but are
More suject then the poorest payes you dutie,
And must obey your fears, your want of sleepe,
Rebellion from your Vassals, wounds even from
Their very tongues, whose quietnesse you sweat for,
For whose dear health you waste, and fright your
Strength to palenesse, and your blood into a frost.
You are not certaine of a friend or servant,
To build your faith upon, your life is but
Your subjects murmur, & your death their sacrifice;
When looking past your selfe, to make them blest
In your succession, which a wife must bring you;

You may give up your libertie for a smile
As I ha' done, and in your bosome cherish
More danger then a warre or famine brings,
Or if you have a sonne—my spirits faile me
At naming of a sonne.

PRINCE [Coming forward]
Oh my deare father.

KING
Ha! do not fright me in my tears, which should
Be rather blood, for yeelding to thy death,
I have let fall my penitence, though I was
Counsel'd by him whose truth I now suspect,
In the amaze and puzzle of my state—

PRINCE
Dear sir, Let not one thought afflict you more,
I am preserv'd to be your humble sonne still,
Although Gotharus had contriv'd my ruine,
'Twas counterplotted by this honest Captaine.

KING
I know not what to credit, art Turgesius?

PRINCE
And do account your blessing, and forgiveness
(If I have err'd) above the whole worlds Empire
The Armie sir is yours.

OLAUS
Upon conditions—

PRINCE
Good sir—and all safety meant your person.

OLAUS
Right, but for your gipsie Queen, that Cocatrice.

KING
She's lost.

OLAUS
The Devil find her.

KING
She's false.

OLAUS
That Gentleman
Jack in a Box, if he could speake,
Would cleare that point.

KING
Forgive me gentle boy.

PRINCE
Dear sir no more.

AQUINUS
Best dismiss these Gentlemen.

OLAUS
The Princes bountie, now you may go home;
And d'ee heare, be drunk to night, the cause requires it.

PRINCE
We'l shew our selves good subjects.

OMNES
Heaven bless the King and Prince, and the good Duke.

[Exeunt.

KING
My comforts are too mighty, let me poure
More blessings on my boy.

PRINCE
Sir, I am blest
If I stand faire in your opinion.

KING
And welcome good Olaus.

OLAUS
Y'are deceiv'd,
I am a Ruffian, and my head must off
To please the Monkey Madam that bewitch'd you,
For being too honest to you.

KING
We are friends.

OLAUS
Upon condition that you will —

KING
What?

OLAUS
Now have I forgot what I would have,
Oh that my Ladie Circe that transform'd you,
May be sent — whether? I ha' forgot agen,
To the Devil, any whether, far enough:
A curse upon her, she troubles me both when
I think on her, and when do I forget her.

[Enter **ALBINA**.

KING
Gotharus wife, the sorrowful Albina.

ALBINA
If pittie dwell within your royal bosome,
Let me be heard; I come to find a husband,
Ile not believe what the hard hearted rebels
Told me, that he is dead, (they lov'd him not
And wish it so) for you would not permit
His murder here. You gave me, sir, to him
In holy marriage, i'le not say, what sorrow
My poor heart since hath been acquainted with,
But give him now to me, and i'le account
No blessing like that bountie; where, oh where
Is my poor Lord? none tell me? are you all
Silent, or deaf as Rocks? yet they sometimes
Do with their hollow murmurs, answer men.
This does increase my fears, none speak to me?
I aske my Lord from you sir, you once lov'd him,
He had your bosome, who hath torne him thence?
Why do you shake your head? and turn away?
Can you resolve me sir? the Prince alive?
Whose death they would revenge upon Gotharus.
O let me kisse your hand, a joy to see
You safe, doth interrupt my griefe, I may
Hope now my Lord is saf too, I like not
That melancholly gesture; why do you make
So dark your face, and hide your eies, as they
Would shew an interest in sorrow with me.
Where is my Lord? can you or any tell me
Where I may find the comfort of mine eies,
My husband; or but tell me that he lives,
And I will pray for you—then he is dead
Indeed I feare.

PRINCE
Poor Ladie.

AQUINUS
Madam be comforted.

ALBINA
Why that's well said, I thank you gentle sir,
You bid me be comforted, blessing on you,
Shew me now reason for it, tell me something
I may believe.

AQUINUS
Madam, your husbands dead.

ALBINA
And did you bid me sir be comforted
For that? oh you were cruel dead? who murdered him?
For though he lov'd not me in life, I must
Revenge his death.

PRINCE
Alas you cannot.

ALBINA
No?
Will not heaven heare me think you? for i'le pray
That horror may pursue the guiltie head
Of his black murderer, you doe not know
How fierce and fatall is a widowes curse;
Who kil'd him? saie.

AQUINUS
We know not.

ALBINA
Y'are unjust.

PRINCE
Pursue not sorrow with such inquisition
Ladie.

ALBINA
Not I? who hath more interest?

KING
The knowledge of what circumstance depriv'd him

Of life, will not availe to his return;
Or if it would, none here know more, then that
He was brought hither dead in that inclosure.

ALBINA
Where?

AQUINUS
In that Coffin Ladie.

ALBINA
Was it charitie
Made this provision for him? oh my Lord
Now may I kisse thy wither'd lip, discharge
Upon thy bosome a poor widowes tears;
There's something tempts my heart to shew more dutie,
And wait on thee to death, in whose pale dresse
Thou dost invite me to be reconcil'd.

KING
Remove that Coffin.

ALBINA
Y'are uncharitable;
Is't not enough that he is rob'd of life
Among you, but you'l rob me of his bodie?
Poor remnant of my Lord; I have not had
Indeed so many kisses a great while,
Pray do not envie me, for sure I sha'not
Die of this surfet, he thought not I was
So neare to attend him in his last and long
Progresse, that built this funerall tenement
Without a roome for me; the sad Albina
Must sleepe by her dead Lord, I feel death coming,
And as it did suspect, I durst not look
On his grim visage, he has drawn a curtaine
Of mist before my eyes.

[Swoons.

KING
Look to the Lady.

PRINCE
Look to Albina, our Physicians!

[Enter **PHYSICIANS**.

There is not so much vertue more i'th Kingdome:
If she survive this passion, she is worth
A Prince, and I will court her as my blessing.
Say, is there hope?

PHYSICIAN
There is.

PRINCE
Above your lives preserve her.

PHYSITIAN
With our best art and care.

[Exit with **ALBINA**.

OLAUS
She has almost made me woman too; but
Come to other businesse.

[Enter **QUEEN MARPISA**.

AQUINUS
Is not this the Queen?

OLAUS
The Queen of hell! Give her no hearing, but
Shoot, shoot her presently without more repentance,
There is a leacherous Devil in her eye,
Give him more fire, his hell's not hot enough,
Now shoot.

PRINCE
Be temperate good sir.

QUEEN MARPISA
Nay let his cholerick highness be obey'd.

AQUINUS
She is shot-free.

QUEEN MARPISA
The Prince alive? where is Gotharus?

OLAUS
Your friend that was.

QUEEN MARPISA

It is confest.

OLAUS
Your Stallion.

QUEEN MARPISA
He has more titles sure.

OLAUS
Let but some strangle her in her own haire.

QUEEN MARPISA
The office will become a noble hangman.

OLAUS
Whore—

QUEEN MARPISA
Ile not spend my breath upon thee,
I have more use on't, does Gotharus live?

AQUINUS
You may conjecture Madam, if you turn
Your eyes upon that object.

QUEEN MARPISA
It has wrought then.

KING
What has wrought?

QUEEN MARPISA
His Physick sir,
For the state Megrim.
A wholsome poyson, which in his poor feares,
And fainting when the Rebels first pursu'd him,
It was my happinesse to minister
In my poor boyes revenge, kil'd by his practise.

PRINCE
Poyson'd.

OLAUS
She is turn'd Doctor.

QUEEN MARPISA
He becomes
Deaths pale complexion, and now I'm prepar'd

PRINCE
For what?

QUEEN MARPISA
To die.

OLAUS
Prepar'd to be damn'd, a seven years killing
Will be too little.

QUEEN MARPISA
I pitty your poor rage,
I sha'not stay so long, nor shall you have
The honour sir to kill me.

OLAUS
No, let me trie.

QUEEN MARPISA
Ha! Ha!

OLAUS
Dost thou laugh Helcat?

QUEEN MARPISA
Yes, and scorne all your furies, I was not
So improvident, to give Gotharus all
My cordiall, you may trust the operation,
Here's some to spare, if any have a mind
To taste, and be assur'd, will you my Lord?
'Twill purge your choler rarely.

OLAUS
Ile not be your patient I thank you.

QUEEN MARPISA
This box was ever my companion,
Since I grew wicked with that Polititian,
To prevent shameful death, nor am I coy
To pleasure a friend in't.

OLAUS
Devils charity.

QUEEN MARPISA
It works with method, and doth kill discreetly
Without a noise, your Mercury is a rude

And troublesome destroyer to this medicine;
I feel it gently seize upon my vitals,
'Tis now the time to steale into my heart.

KING
Hast thou no thought of heaven?

QUEEN MARPISA
Yes, I do think
Sometimes, but have not heart enough to pray;
Some vapour now rises 'twixt me and heaven,
I cannot see't, lust and ambition ruin'd me:
If greatnesse were a priviledge i'th other
World, it were a happiness to die a Queen,
I find my conscience too late, 'tis bloody,
And full of staines, oh I have been so wicked,
'Twere almost impudence to aske a pardon,
Yet for your own sakes pitty me; survive
All happie, and if you can, forgive, forgive.

[Dies.

KING
Those accents yet may be repentance.

PRINCE
See's dead.

KING
Some take their bodies hence.

PRINCE
Let them have burial.

[Exeunt **SOULDIERS** with the bodies of **GOTHARUS** and **QUEEN MARPISA.**

KING
'Tis in thee Turgesius
To dispose all, to whom I give my Crown;
Salute him King by my example.

PRINCE
Stay,
Upon your dutie staie, will you be traytors,
Consent your lawful King should be depos'd?
Sir, do not wound your Son, and lay so great
A staine upon his hopeful, his green honour,
I now enjoy good mens opinions,

This change will make 'em think I did conspire,
And force your resignation, were it still
By justice and your selfe, it shall not touch
My brow, till death translate you to a Kingdome
More glorious, and you leave me to succeed,
Better'd by your example in the practise
Of a Kings power and dutie.

KING
This obedience
Will with excess of comfort kill thy father,
And hasten that command thou wouldst decline.

PRINCE
Receive this Captain, and reward his faith
To you and me.

[Presents **AQUINUS**.

KING
Be Captaine of our guard.
And my good Uncle, to your eare I leave
The Souldiers, let the largesse speak our bountie
And your love.

OLAUS
I, this sounds well fellow Souldiers,
Trust me beside your pay for the Kings bountie.
Within Sol.
Heaven preserve
The King and Prince.

OLAUS
Not a short prayer for me?

OMNES SOLDIERS
Heaven bless the Duke, heaven bless the Duke.

OLAUS
Why so, money will do much.

KING
A bright daie shines upon us, come my sonne,
Too long a stranger to the Court, it now
Shall bid thee wellcome, I do feel my years
Slide off, and joy drown sorrow in my tears.

[Exeunt **OMNES**.

The following includes years of first publication, and of performance if known, together with dates of licensing by the Master of the Revels if available.

TRAGEDIES
The Maid's Revenge (licensed 9th February 1626; printed, 1639)
The Traitor (licensed 4th May 1631; printed, 1635)
Love's Cruelty (licensed 14th November 1631; printed, 1640)
The Politician (acted, 1639; printed, 1655)
The Cardinal (licensed 25th May 1641; printed, 1652).

TRAGI-COMEDIES
The Grateful Servant (licensed 3rd November 1629 as The Faithful Servant; printed 1630)
The Young Admiral (licensed 3rd July 1633; printed 1637)
The Coronation (licensed 6th February 1635, as Shirley's, but printed in 1640 as a work of John Fletcher)
The Duke's Mistress (licensed 18th January 1636; printed 1638)
The Gentleman of Venice (licensed 30th October 1639; printed 1655)
The Doubtful Heir (printed 1652), licensed as Rosania, or Love's Victory in 1640
The Imposture (licensed 10th November 1640; printed 1652)
The Court Secret (printed 1653).

COMEDIES
Love Tricks, or the School of Complement (licensed 10th February 1625; printed under its subtitle, 1631)
The Wedding (ca. 1626; printed 1629)
The Brothers (licensed 4th November 1626; printed 1652)
The Witty Fair One (licensed 3rd October 1628; printed 1633)
The Humorous Courtier (licensed 17th May 1631; printed 1640).
The Changes, or Love in a Maze (licensed 10th January 1632; printed 1639)
Hyde Park (licensed 20th April 1632; printed 1637)
The Ball (licensed 16th November 1632; printed 1639)
The Bird in a Cage, or The Beauties (licensed 21st January 1633; printed 1633)
The Gamester (licensed 11th November 1633; printed 1637)
The Example (licensed 24th June 1634; printed 1637)
The Opportunity (licensed 29th November 1634; printed 1640)
The Lady of Pleasure (licensed 15th October 1635; printed 1637)
The Royal Master (acted and printed 1638)
The Constant Maid, or Love Will Find Out the Way (printed 1640)
The Sisters (licensed 26th April 1642; printed 1653).
Honoria and Mammon (printed 1659)

DRAMAS
A Contention for Honor and Riches (printed 1633), morality play
The Triumph of Peace (licensed 3rd February 1634; printed 1634), masque
The Arcadia (printed 1640), pastoral tragicomedy

St. Patrick for Ireland (printed 1640), neo-miracle play
The Triumph of Beauty (ca. 1640; printed 1646), masque
The Contention of Ajax and Ulysses (printed 1659), entertainment
Cupid and Death (performed 26th March 1653; printed 1659), masque